CW00499441

CHARLES DICKENS

Bleak House

Retold by Margaret Tarner

UPPER LEVEL

Founding Editor: John Milne

The Macmillan Readers provide a choice of enjoyable reading materials for learners of English. The series is published at six levels – Starter, Beginner, Elementary, Pre-Intermediate, Intermediate and Upper.

Level control

Information, structure and vocabulary are controlled to suit the students' ability at each level.

The number of words at each level:

Starter	about 300 basic words
Beginner	about 600 basic words
Elementary	about 1100 basic words
Pre-Intermediate	about 1400 basic words
Intermediate	about 1600 basic words
Upper	about 2200 basic words

Vocabulary

Some difficult words and phrases in this book are important for understanding the story. Some of these words are explained in the story and some are shown in the pictures. From Pre-Intermediate level upwards, words are marked with a number like this: ...³. These words are explained in the Glossary at the end of the book.

Contents

1

The Court Of Chancery

London in November. The Lord Chancellor is in his High Court of Chancery. Ada Clare, Richard Carstone and Esther Summerson meet the Lord Chancellor. He tells the three young people that they are going to live at Bleak House.

London, 1852. London in November. It was cold winter weather. There was mud in the streets. Dogs were covered in mud, almost drowned in it. Horses, pulling carriages[3] through the city streets, were splashed up to their eyes. Shivering crossing-sweepers[3] tried hard to sweep back the mud and dirt on the busy roads.

There was fog too. The fog was everywhere. It came up the river and down the river. Fog covered the boats on the river and filled the boatmen's eyes. Street lamps sent a pale, yellow light through the thick, foggy air.

Cold, mud and fog filled the streets of London. And the fog was thickest and the mud was deepest near Lincoln's Inn, the very heart of London. The Lord High Chancellor was there, sitting in his High Court of Chancery[1].

Some of the fog and the mud had got into the courtroom too. Perhaps a little fog and mud had got into the minds of the people in the High Court of Chancery.

Chancery had ruined[5] many men and driven others to madness. Whole families had been destroyed by Chancery and Chancery had brought great houses to decay and destruction. The streets of London were dark that day and in the Court of Chancery

London. London in November. It was cold winter weather.

it was darker.

The case before the Court was the case of Jarndyce and Jarndyce, and that case had never done anyone any good. The lawyers had lost all interest in Jarndyce and Jarndyce many years before. Whole families had been born and died during the history of Jarndyce and Jarndyce. Pretty young wards of court[1] had grown old and sad; strong young men had lost hope, and still the case had not ended. Over the years, Jarndyce and Jarndyce had slowly ruined the lives of many innocent people.

No decision was reached on that foggy afternoon. The Lord Chancellor moved a little on his high seat.

'We will continue the case on Wednesday fortnight,' said the Lord Chancellor. He stood up. The court stood up. But the Lord Chancellor had something more to say. He looked down at a paper in his hand. Then he spoke.

'The young girl, Ada Clare, and the young man, Richard Carstone, are claimants[1] in Jarndyce and Jarndyce. I am making them wards of court. They will stay at Bleak House with John Jarndyce. I believe he is their cousin. I shall see them in my private room now.'

The Lord Chancellor left the court. The lawyers left too. A little old woman, seated in the front of the court, left last of all. The lights were put out and the doors were locked.

How much better for the wards of court if those doors had never opened again. How much better if Richard Carstone and Ada Clare had never heard of Jarndyce and Jarndyce and had never seen the High Court of Chancery.

Richard and Ada were in the Chancellor's private room standing by the smoky fire trying to keep warm. There was a quiet girl with a calm face and smooth, dark hair standing close to Ada. This was Esther Summerson. Esther was not a ward of court, but the case of Jarndyce and Jarndyce was going to darken her life too. The three young people looked up as the Lord Chancellor came into the room.

6

'Miss Clare?' said the Lord Chancellor to his clerk. 'Who is Miss Ada Clare?'

'This is Miss Clare,' said the clerk.

Ada was a beautiful young girl with golden hair. What was such a young and beautiful girl doing in that dark place?

'You are to stay at Bleak House,' said the Lord Chancellor, looking at his papers, 'with your cousin, John Jarndyce.'

The Lord Chancellor looked up again. 'Richard Carstone?'

Richard Carstone was the young man standing by the fire. His face was eager and happy. As yet, Jarndyce and Jarndyce had not darkened it. Richard bowed.

'And this,' said the clerk, turning to the other girl, 'is Miss Esther Summerson. She will be a companion for Miss Clare and live at Bleak House too.'

The Lord Chancellor nodded.

'Very well. You will all go to stay at Bleak House. But you are to stay in London for tonight.'

'Yes, sir,' Richard Carstone answered. 'We are to stay at the house of Mrs Jellyby.'

'Ah, yes,' he said. The Lord Chancellor had heard of Mrs Jellyby. 'She is a remarkable woman. My clerk will tell you the way to her house.'

The Lord Chancellor left the room and he was soon lost in the fog and darkness. The clerk told the three young people the way to Mrs Jellyby's house and left them outside the court. As they turned to go, a little old woman came smiling out of the shadows.

'The wards-in-Jarndyce,' she said. 'I am very happy to meet you. I am Miss Flite. Everyone knows me here. I come to the court every day. I am waiting for a judgement[1]. It is good to see youth and beauty here.' And Miss Flite smiled again and bowed.

'She's mad,' whispered Richard to Ada, not thinking that the old woman would hear him. But she did.

'That's right, young gentleman,' said Miss Flite. 'I'm mad, quite mad. I was once a ward myself, like you. I was not mad

7

then. I had youth, hope and perhaps a little beauty. But they have all gone. I have come to this court every day for many years. I am waiting for a judgement. But it is a long time. Goodbye, my dears. You will always find me in court.'

The old lady turned and walked quickly away. The fog covered her.

'Poor creature[5],' said Esther softly and took Ada by the hand.

The three young people moved away from Lincoln's Inn towards Chancery Lane and Mrs Jellyby's house. A poor crossing-sweeper stood with his broom, waiting to make a way for them through the mud and dirt of the road. Dirty and ragged, he shivered with cold and gladly accepted a little money from Richard. Jo was this boy's name and he was one of the poorest of the London poor. Jo looked at the three young people as, laughing and talking together, they walked away into the fog and darkness.

2

The Dedlocks At Home

The Dedlocks are in their country-house, Chesney Wold. Mr Tulkinghorn, Sir Leicester Dedlock's lawyer, shows the Dedlocks some papers about Jarndyce and Jarndyce. Lady Dedlock is taken ill.

While darkness and fog were covering London, it was raining in Lincolnshire. The rain fell and the rain dripped from the roof of Chesney Wold, the country-house of the Dedlocks. Sir Leicester Dedlock was a proud old man. He was sometimes troubled by illness. Lady Honoria Dedlock, his wife, was a proud and beautiful woman.

My Lady Dedlock had come to Chesney Wold to get away from the fogs of London. But she found Lincolnshire very dull. Water covered the parkland. Even the trees seemed wet through. The animals in the park and in the stables were cold and miserable.

As darkness fell, the rain dripped on the pavement of the terrace in front of the great house. People called this terrace the Ghost's Walk. Sometimes footsteps were heard on this pavement. They belonged to another Lady Dedlock who had died many years before. She had brought disgrace[5] to her family before she died. Now, when death or disgrace was coming to the Dedlock family, these footsteps were heard on the hard stones.

Had Lady Dedlock ever heard those footsteps? No one knew. Her face – no longer young, but still beautiful – never showed her thoughts. Lady Dedlock was a very proud woman and she had married an even prouder man.

Lady Dedlock was sitting in the library on this wet November evening. She was sitting by the fire, shading her face with a

9

Chesney Wold, the country-house of the Dedlocks.

beautiful white hand. Sir Leicester was sitting in the library too, his proud face half in shadow. He often looked at Lady Dedlock. Lady Dedlock was difficult to please, but Sir Leicester always tried hard to please her.

There was a third person in the room. This man was often at Chesney Wold and often at Sir Leicester's London house. He was an old man and he was dressed, as he always was, in dull, black, old-fashioned clothes. His name was Tulkinghorn. He was Sir Leicester's lawyer. Mr Tulkinghorn had brought some of the darkness of Chancery to Chesney Wold, for Lady Dedlock was also a claimant in the case of Jarndyce and Jarndyce.

'My Lady's case has been discussed again in Court, has it, Mr Tulkinghorn?' said Sir Leicester. My Lady was too proud to ask the question for herself.

'Yes, the case has been discussed again,' Mr Tulkinghorn replied.

'I suppose nothing has been decided,' said my Lady.

'Nothing important has been decided,' said Mr Tulkinghorn.

'Nor ever will be,' said my Lady.

'I have brought some papers with me. Perhaps you would like me to read them to you,' said Mr Tulkinghorn. He placed the papers on the small table near Lady Dedlock, put on his spectacles and began to read.

'In Chancery. Between John Jarndyce . . .'

My Lady moved in her chair. She looked down at the papers on the table.

'Who copied these papers?' she said, speaking more quickly than usual.

Mr Tulkinghorn stopped reading and looked up in surprise. 'Is that writing called law-hand[2]?' my Lady asked, speaking now in her usual careless way.

'It is not quite the usual law-hand,' said Mr Tulkinghorn. 'I don't think the writer has been copying law papers all his life. Why do you ask?'

My Lady said nothing, but covered her face again with her hand. Mr Tulkinghorn went on reading. His voice was dull and the fire was warm. Sir Leicester closed his eyes.

Suddenly Mr Tulkinghorn stood up.

'Sir Leicester, I'm afraid my Lady is ill.'

'Faint,' said my Lady in a whisper. Her face was white. 'I am faint. Take me to my room.'

Bells were rung. Servants were called. Her favourite maid– a pretty young girl called Rosa – helped Lady Dedlock from the room. Sir Leicester went out with them and returned some time later to the library.

'My Lady will be better soon,' said Sir Leicester. 'Please go on reading, Mr Tulkinghorn. The weather is very bad. My Lady gets bored[5] down here. But she has never fainted before.'

Mr Tulkinghorn did not reply to Sir Leicester, but looked again at the writing on the papers before he started to read.

Darkness had come to Chesney Wold. The rain was still falling. Mr Tulkinghorn went on reading. Was there a sound on the terrace? Could footsteps be heard on the Ghost's Walk? Were death or disgrace coming near the Dedlock family? Lady Dedlock heard the footsteps as she lay silently in her great bedroom. Perhaps even Mr Tulkinghorn heard them.

———

Mr Tulkinghorn was a regular visitor to Chesney Wold and he had his own small room in the tower. He sat there for a long time that night thinking about Lady Dedlock. The handwriting on those papers had made her faint. Had she seen the writing before? Did she know the man who had copied those papers?

Mr Tulkinghorn was an old man and he knew many secrets. They were not his secrets and he did not talk about them. But when he knew anyone's secret, he had power over that person. Did Lady Dedlock, that proud beauty, have a secret?

Mr Tulkinghorn rose early the following morning. He walked

for some time on the flat roof of the tower. He was still thinking about Lady Dedlock. She had a secret. He was sure of that. Mr Tulkinghorn was going to find out what the secret was. First of all, he must find the man who had copied those papers.

When Mr Tulkinghorn decided to do something, that thing was soon done. He left Chesney Wold early, without seeing Sir Leicester or Lady Dedlock again. In a few hours, Mr Tulkinghorn was in London. He began to ask questions and very soon some of those questions were answered.

3

Mr Krook's Rag And Bottle Shop

Ada, Esther and Richard stay with Mrs Jellyby. They walk through the streets of London. They talk to Miss Flite and visit her room in Mr Krook's house. They leave London for Bleak House. Mr Tulkinghorn visits Mr Krook.

Although the weather was cold and there was still a little fog in the streets of London, Ada and Esther got up early. This was the first time they had been in London and they wanted to see the great city. They found Richard ready to go out.

'Glad to see you, my dear cousin,' Richard said to Ada. 'I hope your bed wasn't as hard as mine. Mrs Jellyby's house is really not very comfortable, is it? Where shall we go?'

'Anywhere,' answered Ada. 'Everything is new to us. What do you think, Esther?'

The three young people walked quickly. They admired the long streets. They watched the busy crowds filling the pavements and the carriages passing by. Shopkeepers were already sweeping out their shops and dirty, ragged creatures were searching among the rubbish.

'Look, cousin,' Richard said suddenly to Ada, 'we cannot escape from Chancery. We have come by another way to the Court itself and here's the old lady again.'

There was Miss Flite, bowing and smiling as before.

'The wards-in-Jarndyce,' she cried. 'Very happy to see you, I am sure. Do come and see my lodging[5]. It's very near. Youth and Hope and Beauty are not often seen there.'

She took Esther's hand and Ada and Richard followed behind. Very soon, Miss Flite left the busy main street and turned up a narrow lane. She stopped suddenly outside a shop over which was written, "Krook, Rag and Bottle Shop."

There were many rag and bottle shops in London, but Krook's was the oldest and the dirtiest. On the dirty shop window were notices which read: "Bones bought." "Waste paper bought." "Old Clothes bought." In one corner was a smaller notice which read: "Copying done with speed and care. Apply Nemo, care of Mr Krook."

The shop was full of rubbish. Everything was bought here, but nothing was sold. There were bags of old papers written in law-hand. There were papers tied with tape, law books and bunches of rusty keys. There were broken boxes full of old rags and there were bags full of human hair.

At the back of the shop sat an old man wearing spectacles and a hairy cap. He was short and twisted, with a rough face. A grey cat with green eyes sat at his feet.

'My landlord[5], Krook,' said Miss Flite.

The old man laughed and held up his candle.

'They call me the Lord Chancellor and they call my shop Chancery. Do you know why? I have so many things here – of so many kinds – and I never let anything go. I like old papers and dust and cobwebs. There's no sweeping, cleaning or repairing here. That's why they call me the Chancellor.'

'My young friends are the wards-in-Jarndyce,' said Miss Flite.

'Ah!' said the old man in surprise. 'The great case of Jarndyce and Jarndyce! I knew Tom Jarndyce. He was often here before he died. He shot himself in this shop where the young lady is standing – the young lady with the beautiful, golden hair.'

Mr Krook smiled unpleasantly at Ada.

'That will do, Krook,' said Miss Flite. 'Come along, my young friends.'

She led the three young people up the stairs. Her room was at the top of the house. It was clean, but had very little furniture.

'I cannot give you anything to eat or drink,' said Miss Flite.

Mr Krook's Rag and Bottle Shop.

'I sometimes find life very difficult. But I am waiting for a judgement. And I have my birds.'

Miss Flite led them to a number of bird-cages hanging near the window.

'They are in prison, poor creatures, and sometimes they die there. But they will all go free when I get my judgement. They need more air, but I can't open the window. I'm afraid Mr Krook's cat will catch them.'

Bells rang in nearby churches. It was time for Miss Flite to go to Court. Ada looked at Richard and he left some money for Miss Flite on a shelf. It was clear that Miss Flite was very poor indeed.

Miss Flite led her visitors downstairs. She stopped on the next floor and pointed at a door.

'The only other lodger[5] lives there,' she whispered. 'He is a law-writer and he calls himself Nemo.'

'Nemo! Why that is Latin for "no one!" ' said Richard in some surprise.

Richard and the two girls left Miss Flite outside the Rag and Bottle shop. Mr Krook and his cat watched them walk away.

'What an adventure for our first morning in London,' said Richard. 'It's a strange world, this world of Chancery. But it will never change us, will it?'

'Never, I hope, cousin Richard,' said Ada gently.

When they got back to Mrs Jellyby's house, Mrs Jellyby was already at work. She was sitting at a large desk covered with papers and the whole room was dirty and untidy. Mrs Jellyby was about forty-five years old. She had long brown hair, and her fine, dark eyes always seemed to be looking at things far away. Mrs Jellyby had a husband who never spoke a word and a number of children dressed in torn and dirty clothes.

'You find me very busy as usual, my dears,' said Mrs Jellyby. 'My work for Africa takes all my time. The natives on the banks of the river Niger must be fed and educated. I think of nothing else.'

Mrs Jellyby had to send a lot of letters to important people

Mrs Jellyby's house.

and her eldest daughter copied them all in good handwriting. This daughter was a most unhappy-looking girl and her hands, face and clothes were covered with ink. The other children were crying because they had had no breakfast. Esther found them a little to eat and took the youngest boy on her knee. Mrs Jellyby did not notice this. Her work for the natives of Africa took all her time.

'What a strange house,' said Ada, when she and Esther were upstairs.

'Yes, it is strange,' Esther said. 'I'm sure that Mrs Jellyby must be a very good woman. She thinks so much about the natives of Africa. And yet, I think it would be better if she helped her own children too.'

At one o'clock, a carriage arrived to take Esther and the wards of court to Bleak House. The Jellyby children cried loudly when the visitors left, but Mrs Jellyby did not seem to notice they had gone.

———

Long before the carriage arrived at Bleak House, a man dressed in black walked into Mr Krook's Rag and Bottle Shop.

'Is your lodger in?' said the man in black.

'Man or woman, sir?' said Mr Krook.

'Man. The man who does the copying.'

Mr Krook looked at his visitor with interest.

'Second floor, sir. Up there,' he said.

Mr Tulkinghorn was, of course, the man in black. He took a candle and climbed the stairs slowly. He knocked on a door. There was no answer. As he opened the door, the candle went out.

The air of the room was bad. The room was small and black with dirt. In one corner stood an old desk. There was no carpet on the floor and no curtain at the window.

On a low bed opposite the window, Mr Tulkinghorn saw a man. He lay there completely still, dressed in shirt and trousers.

19

His hair and beard were long and ragged. His eyes were open.

Mr Tulkinghorn heard a noise behind him and turned. Mr Krook, his cat at his heels, was standing at the door with another candle in his hand. The two men went nearer the bed.

'God save us!' said Mr Tulkinghorn. 'He is dead. Send for a doctor.'

Mr Krook called Miss Flite and she went to get a doctor. Very soon she returned with a dark-haired young man who worked among the poor of the district.

'I have seen this man many times before,' said the young doctor, whose name was Allan Woodcourt. 'He has been buying opium[3] from me for over a year. He has taken too much opium and has died. There is no doubt of that. Has he any family?'

'I was his landlord,' said Krook. 'He told me once that he had no family but me.'

Allan Woodcourt held the candle close to the dead man's face. 'He must have been a handsome man once. I should think he came from a good family.'

'He called himself Nemo,' said Mr Tulkinghorn. 'Now he is "no one" indeed. Hasn't he any papers? There will have to be an inquest[2].'

They found nothing in the room. A policeman was called and for a time Nemo was left in peace.

Mr Tulkinghorn went home to his own rooms. He sat for a long time thinking about Nemo and thinking about Lady Dedlock. Was Nemo part of Lady Dedlock's secret? Mr Tulkinghorn decided that he would tell Lady Dedlock about the death of Nemo. Mr Tulkinghorn would watch Lady Dedlock's face closely. If Lady Dedlock had a secret, Mr Tulkinghorn would find out what that secret was.

4

At Bleak House

Esther makes friends with John Jarndyce and we learn something of Esther's childhood. John Jarndyce explains the Court of Chancery. Esther meets Jenny, the brickmaker's wife. Jenny's baby dies and Esther covers the baby's face with her handkerchief.

The journey by carriage from London to Bleak House took several hours. The roads were bad and the horses were changed[3] more than once.

Neither Ada, nor Richard nor Esther had ever met John Jarndyce. They talked about the owner of Bleak House during their journey. What kind of man was he? What did their new home look like? The name of the house had an unhappy sound.

The moon and the stars were out when the driver suddenly stood up, waved his whip and cried, 'That's Bleak House – there on the hill.'

There was a light shining in one of the windows. The carriage came nearer to Bleak House and stopped at the front door. The door opened at once, a light shone out and a voice cried, 'Ada, my love, Esther, my dear, you are welcome. I am glad to meet you. And you too, Richard. Come in, all of you.'

The gentleman who had spoken these words had grey hair and a handsome, happy face. This was John Jarndyce. Although he was nearly sixty years old, John Jarndyce was strong and stood up straight. His voice was kind and welcoming.

John Jarndyce led the young people into a room with a bright fire. He was soon asking them many questions.

'How did you like the journey? And how did you like

21

'That's Bleak House – there on the hill.'

Mrs Jellyby, my dear?' said John Jarndyce, looking kindly at Ada.

'She works very hard for Africa,' said Ada, 'but . . .'

'We thought,' said Esther quietly, 'that her own children needed care too.'

'That is what I think,' said John Jarndyce, looking very unhappy. 'They need love and help.'

'And that is what Esther gave them,' said Richard. 'Esther looked after them and Esther loved them.'

'Yes, indeed, Cousin John,' added Ada, while Esther laughed and shook her head. 'I thank you for giving me such a dear friend.'

John Jarndyce was a shy man. He was always doing good, but he hated to be thanked for his kindness. He got up quickly.

'Come girls, come Richard. Let me show you your new home.'

Bleak House had a sad name, but John Jarndyce had made the house a cheerful, pleasant place. There were many doors and little passages. One room led to the other in the strangest way. There was Ada's room, Esther's room and Richard's room. All three rooms were furnished in an old-fashioned but very pleasant way. Everything was neat and ready for their new owners. The three young people were delighted.

'I'm glad you like your new home,' said John Jarndyce. 'This house needs young people and so do I. Please make yourselves at home. Dinner will be ready in half an hour.'

Esther looked round her room with great joy. Her life had not been happy and she had never had a room of her own before. Esther was quick and she was soon ready. She had begun to take her clothes from her bags when a maid came into the room. The maid was carrying two large bunches of keys.

'For you, Miss, if you please,' said the maid to Esther. 'They are the housekeeping keys[3].'

Esther looked surprised.

'I was told to bring them to you. Mr Jarndyce's orders, Miss.'

23

Esther was very pleased. John Jarndyce trusted her. He was giving her the keys of the house. He wanted Esther to look after everything. He was telling Esther that she could be useful and helpful at Bleak House.

Esther had never known her parents and she had had very little love in her life. But she tried to forget her unhappy childhood. And now John Jarndyce had decided to look after her. Esther would make a happy home for everyone at Bleak House.

After dinner, Esther went quietly to Mr Jarndyce's own room. She tried to thank him for his kindness to her.

'You needn't thank me,' he said. 'I heard of a good little girl called Esther. She was an orphan[4] and I decided to look after her. She grew up, and I am still her guardian[4] and her friend. We can live happily at Bleak House. We can make a home for our wards-in-Chancery too.'

'Chancery,' said Esther quietly. 'Can you explain the Court of Chancery to me? I am not clever. I do not understand it.'

'I don't know anyone who does understand it,' John Jarndyce answered. 'I can tell you that the case of Jarndyce and Jarndyce is about a will[1]. Or it was at one time. Now the case is about nothing but money.

'Long ago, a man called Jarndyce made a great fortune. And so he made a great will. This will was difficult to understand. Lawyers have been arguing about it ever since. The Court of Chancery has to decide about the money. Every member of the family has to go to Court sometime. No one can escape. I don't like to think about it. My poor-great uncle[4], Tom Jarndyce, thought about the case all the time. In the end, he shot himself.'

'Did he die in Mr Krook's shop?' asked Esther slowly.

'Yes. And he left me all his money. This house was his home. Because he was so unhappy, he called it "Bleak House". It was a very sad place when he lived here.'

24

'Please don't talk about it sir,' said Esther. 'It makes you unhappy, I know.'

'You are right. We will not talk about Chancery again. The word does make me unhappy. And I think you had better call me "Guardian", Esther, my dear. "Sir" is a little too grand for me.'

Esther smiled and thanked John Jarndyce.

The two young girls slept well that night. To them, Bleak House was already a place of happiness and peace. Esther had a home where she could be busy and happy. Ada was content to live with the people she loved.

Richard lay awake for a long time thinking of the future. He was already interested in the Court of Chancery. He thought about the Jarndyce money. One day there must be a judgement. Jarndyce and Jarndyce had already caused unhappiness and madness, but Richard did not think about that.

———

The days passed happily. Ada and Esther soon met some of the people who lived near Bleak House. One of these was a woman called Mrs Pardiggle. She visited the poor families in the district. Poor people need food, clean houses and warm clothes. Mrs Pardiggle did not give them any of these things. Instead, she read books to them and told them to think about God. The poor people really hated Mrs Pardiggle. They did not want her in their houses, but she refused to stay away. She read dull books to these poor people until they were tired and angry.

One afternoon, Mrs Pardiggle visited Ada and Esther at Bleak House.

'The poor need us,' Mrs Pardiggle told Ada. 'We must teach them how to be good. The men drink and the women are dirty. The worst of them are the brickmakers. I am going to visit them now. Come with me now and see them for yourselves.'

Ada and Esther went very unhappily with Mrs Pardiggle to the brickmakers' cottages. The brickmakers stood outside the poor, dark houses. They said rude things about Mrs Pardiggle in loud voices.

Mrs Pardiggle took Ada and Esther into one cottage where a pale young girl with a bruised[5] face was sitting near to a small fire. There was a little child in her arms, lying pale and still. When Mrs Pardiggle left the cottage, Ada and Esther stayed behind to look at the baby. Ada gently put out her hand to touch its face.

'Oh, Esther,' cried Ada. 'Look at the poor, little thing. It's dead.'

Esther took the baby from its mother's arms and laid it on the bed. She took out her handkerchief and gently covered the baby's face. Esther and Ada tried to comfort Jenny, the dead child's mother. Then they left Jenny alone with the dead child. Esther held up the handkerchief to look once more at the baby's face. It was full of peace. As Esther put back the handkerchief, her tears fell upon it.

Esther took out her handkerchief and covered the baby's face.

5

Tom-All-Alone's

Lady Dedlock returns to London. We learn about Jo, the poor crossing-sweeper. Jo helps a lady and she gives him a piece of gold.

My Lady Dedlock was very bored at Chesney Wold. Nothing interested her. Sir Leicester was ill in bed. Nothing at Chesney Wold pleased my Lady. She decided to return to London. Perhaps life would be more interesting there. In London, Lady Dedlock could visit fashionable people[5], hear music and see new plays.

So my Lady Dedlock went to stay at the Dedlocks' great house in London and Sir Leicester stayed at Chesney Wold.

The city of London went on with its life as usual. Every day, the city woke early. Many of the people of London were at work long before the sun had reached the busy streets.

But there were some streets in London where the sun never came. They were black, dirty streets where it was dangerous to walk. Many years before, the houses in these streets had been pleasant to live in. But now they were black with dirt, the wood was rotten and the windows with no glass in them stared like blind eyes. The stone steps in front of the houses were slippery and green with damp[5].

These houses were in Chancery, of course. Ruined[5] and broken, they were waiting for a judgement. Sometimes one of the houses fell with a terrible crash and a cloud of black dust. But many poor people still lived in these dreadful streets. They had nowhere else to live.

The oldest, dirtiest street, with the blackest, dirtiest houses was called Tom-All-Alone's. Nobody knew who Tom had been, but he must have been in Chancery.

Poor people crowded into Tom-All-Alone's like rats into holes. Every miserable room was full. The poorest of these people was Jo, the crossing-sweeper. Jo knew nothing. He knew that his name was Jo, but he did not know who had given him that name. He had never been to school. All he had was a broom. Jo used his broom to keep his crossing clean. The money Jo earned from sweeping his crossing kept him alive.

Jo knew nothing, but some people had been asking him questions. Nemo, Mr Krook's lodger, had sometimes spoken to Jo and given him a little money. When Nemo died, people asked questions about him at the inquest. Someone found Jo, but he could tell them nothing about Nemo. Mr Tulkinghorn spoke to Jo, but Jo could tell him nothing. All Jo would say was, 'He was very good to me.'

And so Nemo was buried in a dreadful old burial-ground[3], not far from Tom-All-Alone's. Every day, Jo took his broom and swept the steps of the burial-ground. He did this for the man who had been kind to him.

On this London morning, Jo left Tom-All-Alone's as usual. He went through the busy streets, seeing everything, but understanding nothing.

Jo passed shops with their different signs. Jo saw people reading newspapers and letters as they hurried along. It all seemed strange to Jo because Jo could not read. Jo heard a band playing as he went along. Horses and dogs heard it too. Jo understood the music no more than the animals did.

People like Mrs Jellyby helped the poor people of Africa. Why didn't they help Jo? Jo himself did not know the answer to that question. His life was his broom, his crossing and Tom-All-Alone's.

London's day went on as usual. Jo worked at his crossing, sweeping aside the dirt of the London street. Darkness came and rain began to fall. Jo worked on. Lights went on in shops and offices.

. Mr Tulkinghorn sat in his office, working as usual. He was busy and did not stop to look out of his window. If he had looked out into the street, he would have seen a woman hurrying by. She was neatly and plainly dressed. Her face was covered with a veil[3] and her eyes looked down at the ground. She looked like a lady's servant[3] and she walked through the muddy streets with neat, quick steps. She reached Jo's crossing and spoke to Jo in a clear voice.

'Come here.'

Jo followed the lady into a quiet corner.

'Are you the boy who was at the inquest? Tell me.'

'Was the boy's name Jo?' asked the crossing-sweeper.

'Yes,' replied the lady quickly.

'Then that's me,' said Jo.

'Tell me about the man who died,' the lady ordered. 'Was that man very poor?'

'Oh yes,' said Jo, 'oh yes, my lady.'

'Don't call me that; I am a servant.'

Jo knew very little, but he knew that she was not a servant.

The lady had not finished asking her questions.

'Do you know where that man lived and the place where he was buried?'

Jo nodded.

'Take me to those places,' said the lady. 'Go on now, walk in front of me. Don't look behind you. I will give you more money than you have ever seen before. Go on.'

Jo took up his broom without a word and moved through the mud of the dark streets. He stopped first outside Mr Krook's Rag and Bottle Shop.

'He lived here,' said Jo.

'Which room?'

'In the back, up there. You can see the window from this corner. He died there.'

Jo walked on. The streets became darker and the mud was deeper. He reached the steps and the iron gate of the old burial-ground. The lady stood back in horror.

'Why are you stopping here?' she said.

'He was put there,' said Jo.

'Where? In that dreadful place?'

'There,' said Jo, pointing. 'Among the bones, there. I could show you with my broom if the gate was open. But it's always locked. Look! There goes a rat!' And Jo pointed at it with his broom.

The lady stared at Jo.

'Is this dreadful place a burial-ground?' she asked.

'I know they put him there, that's all,' said Jo. 'But don't ask me what they call it. I know nothing.'

The lady took off her glove to get some money from a small bag. Jo saw some bright rings on her smooth, white hand.

The lady dropped some money into Jo's hand and said, 'Show me the place again.'

Jo pushed his broom through the iron bars of the gate trying to point out the place where Nemo was buried. When he turned round again, the lady had gone.

Jo looked at the money in his hand. He took it to a light. It was a piece of gold. Jo put the gold in his mouth for safety. Then, taking up his broom, he swept the steps to the burial-ground with his usual care.

———

That night, long after Jo had gone back to his poor room at Tom-All-Alone's, Lady Dedlock walked down the steps of her house and into her carriage. Beautifully dressed and wearing her

'Is this dreadful place a burial-ground?'

finest jewels, Lady Dedlock was going to a great dinner in a great house.

Down at Chesney Wold, Sir Leicester could not sleep. That night, the footsteps on the Ghost's Walk were heard louder than ever before.

6

Richard's Search For a Profession

Happy days at Bleak House. Ada and Richard fall in love. The young doctor, Allan Woodcourt, visits Bleak House. Richard decides to be a doctor, but later changes his mind. Allan Woodcourt leaves England.

All through the winter, Esther and Ada continued their happy life at Bleak House. They read together, worked together and the winter days flew by quickly. Sometimes, in the afternoons and evenings, Richard Carstone sat with the two girls.

Richard was a restless young man. Sometimes he read and studied for hours at a time. At other times, he rode through the countryside all day and sat in a chair, doing nothing, all the evening. Richard was always talking about what he was going to do with his life. At first, he thought he might be a sailor. He liked the sea. But Richard always talked about the future in a careless way.

Richard's ideas about life and about money worried John Jarndyce. He spoke to Esther about it.

'Richard has no plans for the future,' he said. 'I am afraid that Chancery is to blame. Richard thinks that he may have a lot of money. He thinks that the case of Jarndyce and Jarndyce will make him rich one day. When I talk to Richard, he listens to me, of course. In fact, he agrees with everything I say. But in a few minutes, he is talking about something else.'

Richard was uncertain about his future, but one thing was certain – his feelings for his cousin Ada.

In the evenings, Esther watched the two cousins talking together. Esther soon saw that Richard was in love with Ada

34

and that Ada loved Richard too. Esther said nothing. She waited until one evening when Ada told her secret.

'Richard says that he loves me dearly and I can hardly believe it.'

'My dear,' said Esther with a laugh, 'I could have told you that weeks and weeks ago.'

'Do you think my Cousin John knows?' said Ada. 'We want to tell him.'

'Unless Cousin John is blind, I am sure he knows already,' Esther answered with a smile. And so he did. John Jarndyce was glad to see the happiness of his two wards. He hoped that Richard's love for Ada would help him to work more steadily and to plan for the future. John Jarndyce agreed to their engagement[4].

That evening there was a small dinner-party at Bleak House. It was a happy time. Ada and Richard were so young and so much in love that they made their friends very happy. The only guest was a young doctor whose name was Allan Woodcourt. He was the same young man who had been called to help Nemo, the poor law-writer. He was a quiet, sensible young man and he sat next to Esther.

Richard had decided to be a doctor, like Allan Woodcourt. He was quite sure that he wanted to be a doctor. He had bought his books and he was going to begin his studies in London as soon as possible.

That evening, Richard talked about the future.

'You must write to me every week, my dear Esther, and tell me how Ada is. You will see how hard I will work. And one day, Esther, you will be my dear Ada's bridesmaid[4]. And if the case does make us rich . . .'

Richard stopped because Ada did not look happy.

'I think we will always be poor, Richard,' Ada told him.

'Well, all I am saying is that the case of Jarndyce and Jarndyce *may* make us rich one day. We must have hope. But if you wish, I will not speak of it any more.'

35

A small dinner-party at Bleak House.

And so the rest of the evening passed in laughter and the greatest happiness. There was love and joy in the house that had once been so unhappy. John Jarndyce was very glad that he had taken the wards-in-Chancery into his house. And he was glad, too, to see the pleasure that Esther gave to her friends.

So Richard Carstone left Bleak House. He was going to live with a successful doctor in London. He was going to learn to be a doctor.

Before he left Bleak House, Richard promised to write to Ada and to Esther. But, as time went on, his letters became fewer and fewer.

Some months later, John Jarndyce received a letter from the doctor who was teaching Richard. In this letter, the doctor said that Richard was not doing well. Richard had worked hard at first, but now he seemed to have no interest in his studies. The doctor also said that Richard was spending far too much money.

Ada and Esther decided to visit Richard in London. They thought that Richard would speak more freely to them than to John Jarndyce. Ada, of course, thought that Richard was right in everything he did. But Esther, in her quiet way, wanted to find out the truth.

When the two girls reached London they went straight to the doctor's house.

'Well, how are you getting on, Richard?' Esther said.

'I get on well enough,' Richard replied. 'But it's all rather dull. Of course, I know I'm only passing the time until the case is finished.'

'I am afraid,' said Esther slowly, 'you will say that about anything you do, Richard.'

'I decided to be a doctor a little too quickly, perhaps,' said Richard. 'I have been thinking that perhaps the Law is more interesting.'

'The Law,' repeated Ada, as though she was afraid of the word.

'If I studied the Law,' Richard went on, 'I could go into Court. I could look after Ada's claim in the case, and mine too. That's worthwhile, you know.'

Esther and Ada could not make Richard change his mind. But he agreed to return with them to Bleak House. John Jarndyce must be told of his ward's change of plan.

Richard was an honest young man. He told John Jarndyce that he had lost interest in being a doctor. He wanted to study the Law.

John Jarndyce hated the Law and was afraid of it, but he listened to what Richard said.

'I have made a mistake, dear cousin,' Richard told him. 'We all make mistakes. But I promise you, and I promise my dear Ada, that I will make a fine lawyer. Believe me, I will.'

Mr Jarndyce sat in silence for a few minutes before he spoke.

'If we must make the change, we will. But for Ada's sake, Richard, we must be careful.'

'Cousin John, I hope you are not angry with Richard,' said Ada.

'No, no, my love,' said John Jarndyce. 'It is very easy to make mistakes. I will help Richard all I can.'

John Jarndyce placed his hands gently on Ada's shoulders, smiled at Richard and walked slowly from the room. Only Esther saw the sadness in his face.

Esther went to her room soon afterwards, but she could not sleep. She took out her sewing[3] and began to work. But she soon found that she had left some thread in a room downstairs. She took a candle and went down. To Esther's surprise, her guardian was still sitting by the fire in his own room. His hand was over his face and he looked very unhappy.

'Esther!' he said in surprise. 'Are you still awake, my dear?'

'I couldn't sleep, so I decided to work,' said Esther. 'You have no trouble, I hope?'

'My dear Esther,' said John Jarndyce. 'No trouble. But I was thinking of you and your story.'

'My story? Have I a story?' said Esther. 'If I have a story, it must be a sad one. My earliest memory is of these words: "Your mother, Esther, was your disgrace and you are hers." ' Esther covered her face with her hands.

'Nine years ago, my dear,' said John Jarndyce, 'I received a letter about you. It was from the woman who had spoken those cruel words. She had brought you up in secret. This woman asked me to finish what she had begun. I agreed. You did not know about it, but I helped you for several years. Now I have the pleasure of my dear Esther here at Bleak House. And how happy my dear Esther makes me!'

'And how happy you make me, my dear Guardian. You are like a father to me.'

'Then I shall say goodnight to you like a father, my dear,' said John Jarndyce, 'Goodnight and sleep well.'

And Esther went up to her room feeling happy because she was loved.

Bleak House had a visitor the next day. He was the young doctor, Allan Woodcourt. He had come to say goodbye to his friends at Bleak House. Allan Woodcourt was going to be a ship's doctor. He was going to sail to India and to China. He would be away for a long time.

All his friends were sorry to see Allan go.

Esther was very busy after saying goodbye to Allan Woodcourt. She worked hard and Ada heard her singing. But Esther's face was sad.

In the evening, Esther went into Ada's room.

'What beautiful flowers,' said Esther. 'Are they from Richard?'

'No, they are not from Richard,' said Ada with a laugh.

'Well,' said Esther. 'You must have two men in love with you.'

'Do these flowers look like a gift from a lover?' said Ada.

'Of course they do, Ada,' Esther replied laughing. 'Who is the man?'

Ada did not answer, but she held the flowers against Esther's dress.

'They are for you, Esther. They were left by somebody who is going far away on a ship. Do they look like a lover's gift, Esther, do they, my dear?'

But Esther, half-laughing and half-crying, had already run out of the room. She did not forget to take the flowers with her.

Ada held the flowers against Esther's dress.

7

Esther Meets Lady Dedlock

Ada, Esther and John Jarndyce visit the home of Mr Boythorn, near Chesney Wold. Esther sees some of the people from Chesney Wold in church and later speaks to Lady Dedlock.

John Jarndyce had a very good friend called Lawrence Boythorn. Mr Boythorn often visited Bleak House. He was a big man with a very loud voice. John Jarndyce had known Lawrence Boythorn for more than forty-five years.

When Lawrence Boythorn visited Bleak House, his loud voice was heard everywhere. He always seemed to be angry. But, in fact, Mr Boythorn was the kindest and most polite of men.

In the summer, Lawrence Boythorn invited John Jarndyce and his wards to stay with him in his house in the country.

Richard, by now, was working in a lawyer's office in London. Lawyers usually take long holidays in the summer, but Richard refused to leave his work. He spent all his time now reading and thinking about Jarndyce and Jarndyce.

Lawrence Boythorn lived near Chesney Wold and Sir Leicester Dedlock was his near neighbour. Mr Boythorn hated the proud Sir Leicester.

In the country, the weather was delightful. The birds sang happily and the fields were full of wild flowers. Late in the afternoon, Ada, Esther and John Jarndyce arrived at the little country town where Mr Boythorn was waiting for them with his own little carriage.

'I am sorry, ladies,' said Mr Boythorn, 'that we cannot go by the shortest way. But that way is through Sir Leicester Dedlock's park and I will never go across that man's ground.'

'Are the Dedlocks down here, Lawrence?' asked John Jarndyce as they drove along.

'That proud man is here, yes,' said Mr Boythorn, 'and his wife, Lady Dedlock, will be here soon. I shall never know why she married him.'

They were soon passing by the park and Chesney Wold could be seen. The house, trees and gardens looked beautiful and peaceful.

Mr Boythorn lived in a pretty little house near Chesney Wold. His little house had bright gardens all round it. The trees were heavy with fruit. All was quiet and peaceful. Even the birds in the garden seemed to sing quietly.

The visitors arrived at the house on a Saturday. On the Sunday morning they walked to the little church in the park.

Inside the church Esther looked round. Most of the people were servants from Chesney Wold. The youngest person there was a pretty girl with dark hair and bright red cheeks. Behind this young girl Esther saw a tall, neatly-dressed woman who looked French. The Frenchwoman was handsome, but her cruel, dark eyes were full of anger and hate.

The bells stopped ringing. The people stood up. Sir Leicester Dedlock, his wife by his side, walked slowly into the church.

Esther looked at Lady Dedlock's proud, beautiful face and, for a moment, Lady Dedlock looked straight into Esther's eyes.

Esther had a strange feeling. For a moment she remembered her unhappy childhood. She remembered the face of the hard woman who had brought her up. Did Lady Dedlock look like this woman? Surely not. And yet Lady Dedlock's face reminded Esther of her own unhappy childhood.

The feeling passed and Esther said nothing to her friends.

All through the following week, the sun shone and the skies were blue. The visitors spent all their time out of doors. They walked slowly, through the woods and sat under the great trees in the park of Chesney Wold.

43

The next Saturday, Mr Jarndyce was walking with Ada and Esther as usual. The weather had become very hot and a storm was near.

Suddenly great drops of rain began to fall. By chance, the friends were near a small cottage. Mr Jarndyce quickly led the two girls inside the little house. They stood by the open door and watched the wind bending the trees. The rain fell. The lightning lit up the dark wood. Then they heard the thunder and felt the new freshness of the air.

'Isn't it dangerous to stand so near the door?'

'Oh no, Esther dear,' said Ada.

Esther looked up in surprise. She had not spoken. Esther turned and saw another woman standing in the shadows. It was Lady Dedlock.

'Have I frightened you?' said Lady Dedlock. She looked at Esther who had gone completely white. But why should Esther be frightened?

'I believe,' said Lady Dedlock, 'that I have the pleasure of speaking to Mr Jarndyce. You were in church on Sunday.'

Lady Dedlock gave Mr Jarndyce her hand. She was graceful and beautiful. Lady Dedlock spoke very politely to Mr Jarndyce.

'I think this is your ward, Miss Clare,' said Lady Dedlock looking at Ada. 'Please introduce me to the other young lady.'

'This is Miss Summerson,' said John Jarndyce. 'I am looking after her too.'

'Has Miss Summerson lost both her parents?' asked my Lady.

'Yes.'

'She is very fortunate to have such a kind guardian.' Lady Dedlock looked at Esther as she spoke.

At that moment a small carriage drew up at the door of the cottage. Two women were inside. Esther had seen both of them in church: the Frenchwoman and the pretty young girl.

Lady Dedlock walked gracefully to her carriage. She was surprised to see the Frenchwoman.

'I did not ask you to come,' Lady Dedlock said to her. 'I sent for Rosa.'

The Frenchwoman got out without a word. The others got into the carriage and drove away.

The Frenchwoman's name was Hortense. She stood for a minute looking after the carriage. There was a look of the greatest hatred on her face. Hortense took off her shoes and stood in the long wet grass. Then, with a look on her face as proud as Lady Dedlock's, she started walking towards Chesney Wold.

Hortense took off her shoes and stood in the long wet grass.

8

Jo Moves On

Summer in London. Jo talks about a lady. Inspector Bucket of the London police has a talk with Mr Tulkinghorn. Mr Bucket brings Jo to Mr Tulkinghorn's rooms.

Back in London, the lawyers were still on holiday. It was the Long Vacation[2]. In Lincoln's Inn, the weather was very hot and the empty streets were dusty. It was the hottest, dustiest Long Vacation that the oldest lawyer could remember.

Thirsty dogs howled for water. The little streets seemed to be on fire. Near Mr Krook's Rag and Bottle Shop, it was so hot that people had taken chairs outside their houses. There sat Mr Krook, outside his shop. His cat, who was never too hot, lay by his side.

Mr Snagsby, law-stationer[2], stood outside his shop near Lincoln's Inn, trying to forget the heat. A hot-looking policeman came down the narrow street, holding a ragged boy by the arm.

The policeman began to speak as soon as he saw Mr Snagsby. 'This boy won't move on[3]. I've told him to move on time after time, but he won't do it.'

'I'm always moving on,' said the boy, wiping his eyes on a ragged sleeve. 'I've been moving on ever since I was born.'

'He won't move on,' said the policeman who had now come up to Mr Snagsby. 'He won't move on, so I'm going to lock him up.'

'Oh, it's Jo,' said Mr Snagsby.

'You do know the boy then, sir,' said the policeman. 'He said he knew you.'

'Yes, I know the poor boy,' said Mr Snagsby, looking sadly at Jo. 'He lives down at Tom-All-Alone's.'

'I'm not sure if he's poor,' said the policeman. 'I found these two silver pieces on him. How did a poor boy get two silver pieces?'

'They are what's left,' said Jo, 'out of a gold coin given to me by a lady. She wore a veil and rings. She asked me to show her the burial-ground.'

'I don't believe that,' said the policeman.

'But it's the truth!' said Jo looking at Mr Snagsby.

'Well,' said Mr Snagsby, who was a kind man, 'I'm sure that Jo will move on if you don't lock him up this time.'

'Move on then,' said the policeman to Jo. 'Take your money and make sure you are five miles away from here before it's dark.'

Later that evening, when Jo was still moving on through the dusty streets, Mr Snagsby visited Mr Tulkinghorn.

Mr Tulkinghorn's windows were open and his rooms were cool. Mr Tulkinghorn sat by the window, drinking his wine, listening to Mr Snagsby's story. Mr Tulkinghorn did not say a word until Mr Snagsby had finished telling him about Jo.

Suddenly Mr Snagsby noticed that there was another person in the room. This person had sat in silence all through the story.

'Don't worry about this gentleman,' said Mr Tulkinghorn to Snagsby, 'I wanted him to hear your story. What do you think about this story, Bucket? Mr Bucket is a detective,' Mr Tulkinghorn added.

'I'd like to question that boy,' said Mr Bucket. 'I'd like you to come with me, Mr Snagsby. I want to ask the boy a few questions, sir. I can see you're a man of business, a man to be trusted. No harm will come to the boy. He'll be back at Tom-All-Alone's by now.'

Mr Bucket stood up and took his hat from the table.

'Now, sir,' he said, 'if you're ready, so am I.'

Mr Bucket led Mr Snagsby out of Tulkinghorn's rooms.

As they walked along, Mr Snagsby noticed that many people seemed to know Mr Bucket. Several rough-looking men looked hard at Mr Bucket and then quickly walked in the other direction. Although Mr Bucket always looked straight ahead, Mr Snagsby was sure he saw everybody.

Very soon, a policeman joined them with a light. The narrow streets were now dark. Black mud and dirty water covered the stones. Bad smells were everywhere.

Mr Bucket at last found the dreadful room which was Jo's usual lodging place.

Jo was not there. But there were two men, in a drunken sleep, and two women who were their wives.

'Now who are you?' asked Mr Bucket. 'I've never seen you before. Your husbands are brickmakers. Am I right?'

'Yes, sir. We don't live in London,' said one of the women. 'We walked up yesterday, looking for work.'

'That's not the way to find work,' said Mr Bucket, looking at the sleeping men.

'That's true, sir,' said the older woman, sadly.

A candle burnt weakly in the thick air. Mr Bucket saw the baby in the younger woman's arms.

'Is it yours, my dear?' he asked her.

'No, sir. Mine died, sir. Not long ago.'

'It's better dead, Jenny,' said the older woman, not unkindly.

'Better dead! Why do you say that?' asked Mr Bucket.

'Why?' said the woman. 'Think about the boy who lives here – he's gone to the doctor for medicine. What life has he got? What life has this baby got?'

At that moment, Jo came in.

'That's Jo,' said Mr Snagsby to Mr Bucket.

In a moment, Jo had given the medicine to the woman. In a moment, Mr Bucket had led Jo from the room. Soon they were walking back through the dark, dirty streets. Soon, Mr Bucket was leading the way up Mr Tulkinghorn's stairs. Mr Bucket had a key and he made quite a lot of noise opening the door.

Mr Tulkinghorn was not in his room. There was not much

light in the room and at first it seemed to be empty. Jo stopped suddenly.

'There she is,' cried Jo. 'The lady I took to the burial-ground.'

A woman moved into the centre of the room.

'Now tell me,' said Bucket. 'How do you know that's the same woman?'

'That's her veil,' replied Jo, 'and the dress is the same.'

'Take off your glove,' Mr Bucket told the woman. 'Now look at her hand. Is it the same?'

'No!' said Jo. 'Those rings are different. The hand is not so white. That's not the hand I saw.'

'Do you remember the voice?' said Mr Bucket. 'Now listen, Jo!'

The woman spoke a few words.

'That's not the voice. It's not a bit like hers. That's her dress and that's her veil, but that's not her voice.'

'Well,' said Mr Bucket. 'We haven't learnt much from you. Take this and off you go.'

Jo took the money and left. Mr Tulkinghorn came back into the room. The woman raised her veil. It was the Frenchwoman, who had walked through the wet grass without her shoes down at Chesney Wold.

'Thank you, Mademoiselle Hortense,' said Mr Tulkinghorn. 'That is all we need from you.'

'I hope you will remember,' said Mademoiselle Hortense, 'that Lady Dedlock has dismissed me. I have no job at present. Mr Tulkinghorn could easily help me.'

'I shall not forget you,' said Mr Tulkinghorn, leading the Frenchwoman to the door and watching her go down the stairs.

'Well, Bucket,' said Mr Tulkinghorn.

'There's no doubt about it. It was the other lady but she was wearing this woman's dress,' said Mr Bucket. 'And now, Mr Snagsby, I'm sure you want to go home.'

'There she is. The lady I took to the burial-ground.'

And Mr Snagsby was soon on his way home thinking about the strange events of the evening.

Long after Mr Snagsby had reached home and gone to bed, Mr Tulkinghorn and Mr Bucket sat talking together. Their voices were very quiet, although there was no one near to hear what they said.

9

Richard Becomes a Soldier

Richard becomes more interested in the case of Jarndyce and Jarndyce. John Jarndyce warns Richard. Richard becomes a soldier.

The summer was nearly over and Esther and Ada were back in Bleak House. Richard was still in London, but he went back to Bleak House quite often.

Richard seemed happy at first and he was working hard. But all his thoughts were about Jarndyce and Jarndyce. He went to the Court every day, just like poor Miss Flite, the little mad woman. Like Miss Flite, Richard talked of only one thing, Jarndyce and Jarndyce.

Esther felt unhappy about Richard. But Ada loved her cousin deeply and saw nothing wrong with Richard's interest in Chancery.

'Well, Richard,' Esther said one day when Richard was at Bleak House, 'are you happy now?'

'Happy? Well, I won't be really happy until the case is decided. And that will be soon. I am sure of that. But these things take a lot of money, you know. I do get into debt a little.'

'Do you owe money, Richard?' Esther asked sadly.

'Yes, I'm afraid I do. But things will be different when the case is decided. I expect a judgement very soon.'

'So you like the Law, then, Richard?' asked Esther, kindly.

'The Law? No, not exactly. In fact, I don't like it at all. I have been working hard at Jarndyce and Jarndyce and have grown tired of the Law. Soon we shall have all the money we want. Until then, there is only one life for me.'

'What do you mean?' cried Esther, looking anxiously at Richard's smiling face.

'The Army, of course. I have decided to live as a soldier – just until the case is settled. It will save me money, you know. That's the best plan.'

Esther felt sad, but she could not change Richard's mind. The case of Jarndyce and Jarndyce was already beginning to darken Richard's life.

John Jarndyce was very unhappy about Richard's latest idea. He sat with Richard for many hours, talking to him and trying to change his mind. He could do nothing. Richard became a soldier.

Before Richard went away, John Jarndyce spoke seriously to him and to Ada.

'Ada, my dear,' he said. 'You must understand that our dear Richard has made a choice for the last time. He has no more money and cannot change his mind again.'

'It is true, sir,' said Richard with a smile, 'that I have spent all my money. But it is also true that one day I shall have more, much more. I expect a judgement . . .'

'Richard, Richard,' cried John Jarndyce, standing up suddenly and putting his hands over his ears. 'For the love of God, do not put any hope or trust in Jarndyce and Jarndyce. It is better to borrow, better to beg, better to die.'

The three young people were frightened at the way that their guardian spoke.

'Ada, my dear,' said John Jarndyce, 'these are strong words of advice. But I live in Bleak House and I have seen many terrible things here. But let's speak no more of that. I have something else to say. I feel that it is wrong for Richard and Ada to be engaged. From now on you must be cousins only. Perhaps one day things will change.'

Richard was silent. Ada spoke first.

'Richard, I am staying here with our dear guardian,' she said.

'We must do what he says. May God be with you, my dear Cousin Richard, wherever you go and whatever you do.'

And so Richard left Bleak House to be a soldier. Richard said goodbye to John Jarndyce in a very cold way. It was clear that Richard was angry with his guardian. He was certain that one day very soon Jarndyce and Jarndyce would make him a rich man. Richard could not awake from his dream.

10

Esther's Illness

Jo leaves London and reaches the brickmakers' cottages. He is very ill. Esther helps Jo and catches his illness. When Esther is better, Miss Flite visits her. Miss Flite speaks about Esther's handkerchief and about Allan Woodcourt's bravery at sea.

One cold, windy night, not long after Richard had left, a message was brought to Bleak House. The message was brought by one of the brickmakers' wives. The brickmakers had found no work in London and had returned to their miserable cottages near Bleak House.

'Please come, Miss,' said the woman to Esther. 'It's a poor boy, Miss. He's very ill.'

Esther dressed herself quickly and followed the woman into the dark night.

It was very cold and the trees shook in the wind. Rain had been falling all day and clouds still covered the sky. Esther stood still for a moment and looked towards London. She felt a change was coming into her life. Somehow she felt a different person, with a different life in front of her.

Esther came to the poor cottage, knocked gently at the door and went in. The air of the room was thick and unhealthy. On the floor, close by the poor fire, a boy sat shaking with cold. He looked up when Esther came into the room. When he saw her face, the boy stood up suddenly.

'I know what she's come for,' cried the boy. 'That's the lady I took to the burial-ground. I don't want to go there again. They might keep me there.'

'Jo, what's the matter?' said Jenny, the brickmaker's wife. 'This is dear Miss Summerson.'

'Is it?' said Jo. 'Is it? She looks like the other lady to me. Not the same clothes, but she's very like, very like.' Esther did not understand Jo, but she could see that he was very ill.

'I have come to help you,' Esther said. 'What's wrong with you?'

'I'm being frozen, then burnt. Frozen and burnt up. My head's tired and my bones ache. I came from London yesterday. They told me to move on, so I moved on down here. I'm moving on now before they catch me.'

Jo stood up and, with his head down, went quickly out of the door and along the dark road.

Esther stayed in the cottage for a little longer. They all loved her and even the rough brickmakers were quieter when Esther was near. One of the boys took Esther part of the way home and then she went on by herself. Very soon, she found Jo. He was sitting by the side of the road and looked at Esther with staring eyes.

'There she is. Coming to take me to the burial-ground. She knows I'm dying.'

Esther was frightened, but she saw that Jo was very ill. Esther helped Jo to his feet and they walked together. When they reached Bleak House, Esther went at once to Mr Jarndyce.

With the help of a servant, Jo was led to a warm shed near the house. Esther went to bed, happy that she had helped the poor boy.

But in the morning, Jo had gone. People searched for Jo for five days, but he could not be found anywhere.

One morning, soon afterwards, Esther woke up feeling very ill. Although the sun was shining brightly, Esther felt deadly cold. She had caught poor Jo's illness, but she was far more ill than he had been. Esther would not allow Ada to look after her. This terrible illness could kill, or completely take away a woman's beauty.

Esther helped Jo to his feet and they walked together.

Esther lay ill for many weeks. In her illness, she thought that she was a child again, unhappy and alone. Days passed, like one long, dark night. Esther had strange and dreadful dreams from which she awoke with tears.

At last, Esther began to get better. One day, she was able to sit up in bed and look around her. For a short time, Esther's illness had made her almost blind. She was happy to look round her room again and see all the pretty things she loved. But something seemed to be missing.

'Are all my pictures here?' Esther asked her maid.

'Every one of them, Miss,' was the reply.

'Something has gone,' said Esther. 'Something has been taken away. Oh, I know what it is – my looking-glass[5].'

Esther thought for a few moments. Then she understood why the looking-glass had been taken away.

Esther touched her thin face with thin, white hands. She felt the scars[5] of her illness. But Esther still had something left; her long, dark hair fell heavily around her scarred face.

And she was still loved by all around her. When John Jarndyce sat by Esther's side a few days later, he was as kind as ever.

Esther asked her guardian about Richard. John Jarndyce's face became very sad.

'The truth is that Richard no longer trusts me. Lawyers have told him that I am his enemy – that I want all the money for myself.

'It is not Richard's fault. This case is slowly changing him. It is like a dreadful illness. But now, I have something more pleasant to tell you. My friend, Lawrence Boythorn, has invited you to stay in his house until you are really well. He is leaving it empty especially for you. And another friend has walked the twenty miles from London, just to see you, dear Esther. She is outside the door now.'

John Jarndyce opened the door, and Miss Flite ran into the room, half-laughing, half-crying.

'My dear Esther, how good to see you. I cannot stop crying. I must borrow a handkerchief from you. I have only law papers in my bag. The lady with the veil took your handkerchief. She went to the brickmaker's cottage. Where the baby died.'

'Yes, I remember,' Esther said slowly. 'It was Jenny's child who died. I left my handkerchief to cover the baby's face.'

'I met poor Jenny in London,' Miss Flite went on. 'Jenny wants you to know that the lady with the veil took your handkerchief. She left some money instead.'

'Who is the lady with the veil?' Esther asked. But Miss Flite did not answer Esther's question.

'I am expecting a judgement very soon,' Miss Flite went on. 'It has been a long time. Many of my family have expected a judgement. My father, my sister, my brother – all dead now. The Court pulls people towards it. They cannot stay away. I know the signs[5], my dear. I have seen the signs begin and seen them end. Esther, my love, I have seen the signs in Richard Carstone's face. Someone must stop him or he'll be ruined.'

Miss Flite looked at Esther for a moment in silence. Then she started to search in her little bag. She found the page of a newspaper and held it up.

'Well, my dear, there has been a terrible shipwreck[5] over in the Indian seas.'

'Mr Woodcourt shipwrecked?' cried Esther in horror.

'Don't worry, my dear,' said Miss Flite. 'He is safe. Many people died in the shipwreck, but Mr Woodcourt saved many lives. Read about it for yourself, my dear.'

Esther read the story with tears of joy in her eyes. She was proud to be the friend of such a brave man.

Esther loved Allan Woodcourt. She had sometimes thought that Allan loved her. But no man would ever marry her now. Her illness had changed her too much. Bleak House would be her home for the rest of her life.

'Well, my dear, there has been a terrible shipwreck.'

11

'I Am Your Unhappy Mother!'

Esther learns the truth about her mother.

After a few days, Esther went to stay in Mr Boythorn's little house. She walked in the woods and fields near Chesney Wold and slowly grew stronger.

Esther often sat in an open part of the woods in front of the Dedlocks' great house. Esther had heard the story of the Ghost's Walk. She often sat looking down at the grey stones where the ghostly footsteps were heard.

One afternoon, Esther was sitting in her usual place. She looked up and saw someone walking through the wood towards her. The path was long and dark. Slowly Esther saw that the person was a woman. It was Lady Dedlock. As Lady Dedlock moved towards her, Esther stood up. She did not know what to do.

Lady Dedlock was walking more quickly than usual. Her arms were stretched out in front of her. There was a look on her face that no one had seen ever before. It was a look that Esther had dreamt of all her life. Esther felt faint and her face went white.

'Miss Summerson,' said Lady Dedlock. 'I have frightened you. You have been very ill, I know.'

The two women sat down. Esther saw that Lady Dedlock was holding something in her hand. It was a handkerchief, the one that Esther had left in Jenny's cottage. Esther looked into Lady Dedlock's face. Esther's heart was beating so fast that she could not speak. With a cry, Lady Dedlock took Esther into her arms and kissed her. Then she fell down on her knees in front of Esther.

'Oh, my child, my child, I am your wicked and unhappy mother! Oh try to forgive me!'

'Do not kneel to me,' Esther replied. 'My heart is full of love and joy. I love you, Mother. I am proud to be your daughter.'

'It is too late, far too late,' said Lady Dedlock. 'We must keep our secret. We must keep it for my husband's sake. Sir Leicester is a proud man and my disgrace would kill him. I am a wicked woman.'

'Our secret will always be safe, dearest Mother.'

'I am afraid of one man,' said Lady Dedlock. 'Mr Tulkinghorn. He is my husband's lawyer. He searches out people's secrets. I think he is searching out mine.'

'Can't you trust this man?'

'I shall never try. I must never let anyone know my secret.'

'Perhaps if Mr Jarndyce knew, he could help us . . .'

'Tell him everything,' said Lady Dedlock. 'Tell him, but do not tell me that you have done so. We cannot meet again. When you hear about the proud Lady Dedlock only you will know your mother's misery.'

Lady Dedlock took Esther in her arms for the last time. Then she turned and walked quickly away along the dark path.

Esther walked slowly home. She carried in her hand a letter that Lady Dedlock had given her.

In her own room, Esther read through the letter many times. The cruel woman who had darkened Esther's childhood had been Lady Dedlock's sister. Esther remembered again the dreadful words, 'Your mother, Esther, was your disgrace, and you are hers.'

Esther burnt the letter. In her sadness, she walked out of the house. She went through the woods and up towards the great house of Chesney Wold. She looked at its old grey stones and walked through the sweet-smelling gardens. Then she walked along a terrace by a long line of windows. She heard her footsteps on the hard stones. Suddenly Esther saw that she was on the Ghost's Walk. Esther turned in fear and ran through the darkened park and back to her own room.

12

Mr Tulkinghorn Gives a Warning

Mr Tulkinghorn tells the Dedlocks a story. The Frenchwoman, Hortense, visits Mr Tulkinghorn.

Two months went by. Lady Dedlock had come back from London to Chesney Wold. The great house was full of people once again.

The cold and proud Lady Dedlock sat by a window in the library looking out at the evening shadows in the park.

A servant told her that Mr Tulkinghorn had arrived and was having dinner. My Lady turned her head for a moment and then looked out of the window again.

After a time, Mr Tulkinghorn came into the room. He bowed to my Lady, shook hands with Sir Leicester and sat down on a chair by a small table. The two men talked about a law case. My Lady did not seem to be listening. A judgement had been given against some poor people who lived nearby. Mr Tulkinghorn began to tell a story about the poor people who had fought against Sir Leicester in the case.

'These people are poor, but they are proud too,' said Mr Tulkinghorn. 'Perhaps my Lady Dedlock would like to hear this story.'

Lady Dedlock sat perfectly still. The lawyer continued.

'One of the poor men in the case had a daughter. His daughter became a servant to a great lady. A really great lady. The lady, who was wealthy and beautiful, was very fond of her pretty young servant.'

Lady Dedlock sat in silence. She knew that she was the lady

in Mr Tulkinghorn's story and that the servant was her own servant, Rosa.

Mr Tulkinghorn continued his story. 'Now this great lady had a secret which she had kept for many years. In early life, this great lady had been engaged to a wild young man, a soldier. They were never married, but she had a child – his child.'

Mr Tulkinghorn looked at Lady Dedlock. She sat perfectly still. She knew that the child in Mr Tulkinghorn's story was Esther, her own child. Mr Tulkinghorn went on.

'The soldier had died. The lady believed that her secret was safe. It was not. It became known and there was great trouble in the lady's house. Her proud husband's unhappiness was very great.

'The point of the story is this. When the young servant's father heard the story, he took his daughter away from the lady's home. He was proud too, you see. He would not allow his daughter in the same house as the great lady who had disgraced her husband.'

There was silence in the darkened room. Lady Dedlock knew that Tulkinghorn was giving her a warning. Rosa was still working in her house as a servant. But if Lady Dedlock's secret became known, Rosa would be taken away. Even a poor man would not let his daughter work in the same house as a lady in disgrace.

Lady Dedlock went out first. Soon afterwards, Mr Tulkinghorn walked slowly up to his room in the tower. As he went up the stairs, he saw that the door to his room was open. There was someone inside.

'Lady Dedlock?'

Lady Dedlock did not speak at first. At last she said, 'Why have you told my story to my husband?'

'Lady Dedlock, it was necessary. I wanted you to know that I knew your story.'

'How long have you known it?'

'I have been asking questions for a long while. A few days ago, I knew that the story was true.'

'Do many people know my story?'

'No, Lady Dedlock. Only yourself and me.'

'You want me to leave this house, leave the man I have disgraced? Would that please you?'

'Your secret would be known at once. And it would kill Sir Leicester. I am thinking only of him.'

'Then I am to stay a prisoner in my own house.'

'In Sir Leicester's house. Yes, my Lady.'

'And I must keep my secret as I have kept it for so many years.'

'Yes, my Lady, as you have kept it for so many years. Nothing must be changed. Do you promise?'

'I do.'

Lady Dedlock stood perfectly still for a few moments. Then she turned, went out of the room and down the stairs.

Mr Tulkinghorn soon went to bed. He had done his work at Chesney Wold. Tomorrow he would return to London.

My Lady walked up and down in her own room like an animal in a cage. Her hands pulled at her long, dark hair. Her body was twisted in pain. Was this unhappy woman the cold and proud Lady Dedlock? No one would have believed it.

———

The following evening, Mr Tulkinghorn was in his own room in Lincoln's Inn. He had opened a bottle of his best wine. Just as he put it on his table, there was a knock at the door.

'Who is it?' said Mr Tulkinghorn as he opened the door.

It was the Frenchwoman.

'Oh, it's you, is it? What do you want?'

Mademoiselle Hortense came into the room. She shut the door before she answered him.

'I have waited a long time to see you, sir.'

My Lady walked up and down like an animal in a cage.

'Have you? If you have anything to say, say it.'

'Sir, you brought me here to meet that boy. You learnt some important secret from that meeting. You did not tell me the secret but you paid me. Oh yes, you paid me. Now look, I give you back your money.'

And the Frenchwoman threw two gold pieces on the floor.

'You must be rich, my friend,' said Mr Tulkinghorn. 'You must be very rich to throw money away.'

'I am rich,' cried Mademoiselle Hortense. 'I am rich in hate. I hate my Lady Dedlock with all my heart. You know that.'

'Have you anything else to say, Mademoiselle?'

'I have no job. Find me a job. If not, use me to hunt her. Use me to disgrace my Lady. That is what you plan to do, I know. I will come here again and again until you do what I want.'

'Mademoiselle. If you visit me once more, you will be locked up. You will go to prison.'

'You cannot do it . . .'

'Yes, I can. Now go, Mademoiselle. Think carefully before you come here again.'

Mademoiselle went down the stairs without looking back. Mr Tulkinghorn shut the door, locked it and went back to his table. He poured some wine into a glass. Then he sat down and drank it slowly.

13

Allan Woodcourt Returns

Esther tells John Jarndyce her mother's secret. John Jarndyce asks Esther to marry him. Richard has spent all his money. Esther visits Richard in London and sees Allan Woodcourt again. The death of Jo.

Esther did not forget her mother. When anyone spoke about Lady Dedlock, Esther was afraid. She was afraid that her mother's secret might become known.

John Jarndyce saw that his dear Esther was very unhappy. When Esther told him her mother's story, he listened with the greatest kindness. He promised to keep the secret.

After Esther had left the room, John Jarndyce sat for a long time thinking quietly. Then he took up his pen and slowly began to write. He wrote a letter to Esther.

It was not a love-letter, but it was written with much love. In the letter, he told Esther that she had made Bleak House a place of great happiness for him. He asked his dear ward to marry him so that his happiness would be complete.

John Jarndyce was much older than Esther, of course. His hair was grey, but he was in good health. With Esther as his wife, John Jarndyce could hope for many years of happiness.

Esther read the letter. After she had read it, she cried. The letter made her happy and thankful, and yet she cried. Then Esther went to her looking-glass. Her face had lost its beauty. Esther was sure that no young man would ever want to marry her.

Esther went to a book and opened it. Between the pages were some dried flowers. They were the flowers that Allan Woodcourt had left for her before he sailed away. Esther looked at them sadly and kissed them. Then she held them to a candle until they were all burnt away.

This was Esther's answer to John Jarndyce's letter. She decided to marry her guardian.

Esther's decision brought much happiness to Bleak House. But one thing troubled this happiness. Richard Carstone now hated his guardian. A kind of madness filled Richard's mind. He was sure that John Jarndyce was trying to ruin him.

Ada, who loved her cousin dearly, continued to write to Richard. But Richard's letters to Ada were very few. At first, he wrote about his new life as a soldier. Then all his letters were about Chancery and about Jarndyce and Jarndyce.

One day, Esther received a letter from London. It was from Richard's own lawyer. Nobody at Bleak House liked this man. They knew that he was not helping Richard. This lawyer told Esther that Richard had no more money. Because of his debts, Richard would now have to leave the Army.

Esther decided to visit Richard alone. She knew that Richard would not speak to John Jarndyce. Esther took with her a letter from Ada. It was full of love and hope for the future.

Esther soon found Richard's poor rooms. They were as near as possible to the dark Court of Chancery. The living-room was cold and untidy. Richard, no longer dressed as a soldier, was sitting at a table covered with papers.

'Look at me, Esther. I am without hope. I have no money left. I am a failure.'

'My dear Richard,' said Esther kindly. 'Remember Ada. She loves you and has sent you this letter. Please read it.'

In the letter Ada offered Richard the little money she had left. She wanted Richard to pay his debts and stay in the Army. Richard read the letter with tears in his eyes.

'Dear Ada is so kind to me,' said Richard, with a strange look. 'But perhaps this is one of John Jarndyce's tricks. He wants to ruin me. Esther, why do you want to marry such a man?'

'Look at me, Esther. I am without hope. I have no money.'

'Richard,' cried Esther, 'you must not say these wicked words.' Esther was angry, but she was sorry for Richard. She saw in Richard's pale young face the madness of Chancery.

Richard wrote a letter to Ada and then walked with Esther back to her coach[3].

As they walked through the busy streets of London, Esther thought sadly of the past. She remembered her first day in London with Ada and Richard. She remembered Richard laughing at little Miss Flite and at her hope of a judgement. Now Richard lived by that same hope. The young man and the old woman had both been changed by the madness of Chancery.

'Look, Esther,' Richard said suddenly. 'Isn't that Allan Woodcourt? He has returned from his sea adventures.'

Esther looked up and saw Allan Woodcourt coming towards them. Esther remembered her scarred face as Allan Woodcourt greeted them. Esther thought that he looked at her sadly. He had noticed the loss of her beauty.

Richard left them for a moment to ask about the coach.

'Richard has changed,' said Allan Woodcourt.

'Chancery has changed him,' Esther replied. 'Richard needs a true friend in London, Mr Woodcourt. If you are staying here, I ask you to be that friend.'

'Miss Summerson,' replied Allan Woodcourt, looking at Esther kindly, 'I promise I will be a true friend to Richard.'

Richard came back. Esther's coach was leaving at once. Allan Woodcourt helped her into her seat and held her hand for a moment. Both young men said goodbye to her.

———

Allan Woodcourt walked back with Richard to his rooms. Then the young doctor walked on slowly through the dark streets. Allan Woodcourt was thinking of Esther. She was still the beautiful woman he loved. He knew nothing about Esther's promise to marry John Jarndyce. But Allan Woodcourt now worked among the poor of London and he was a poor man himself. He could not ask Esther to marry him yet.

No one else was walking in those dark streets. Then Allan noticed a poor woman, half asleep on a doorstep. The young doctor spoke quietly to her and gave her a little money. The woman was Jenny, one of the brickmakers' wives.

Something else was moving in the dreadful street. A ragged figure was crawling close to the dirty wall. It was a young, thin boy, dressed in rags and with wild staring eyes.

Suddenly there was a cry and Jenny began to run after the boy.

'Stop him, stop him!' she cried. Allan, thinking that the boy had stolen some money, followed too. The boy twisted and turned, but at last he was caught.

'Oh Jo,' cried Jenny, 'I have found you.'

'Jo?' repeated Allan Woodcourt. 'You were the boy at the inquest. What have you done?'

Jenny answered the question.

'He gave a bad illness to a sweet young lady, sir. That young lady was a good friend to me. She looked after Jo, but he ran away in the night. The young lady lost all her pretty looks because of this wicked boy.'

Allan Woodcourt looked with horror at the boy who had made Esther so ill. But Jo needed help. Allan found some hot food and drink for him. The young doctor saw that Jo would die very soon. Allan took the poor boy to a clean room where he could rest for the last time.

Jo slept for a little, but every breath made a strange noise in his throat. His eyes opened suddenly.

'I thought,' said Jo, looking round, 'I thought I was back in Tom-All-Alone's. Don't take me there, sir. Am I going to the burial-ground, where I took the lady, sir?'

'Lie down, Jo,' said Allan kindly. 'What burial-ground, Jo?'

'Where they put him. He was very good to me. I took her there. The one with the veil and the rings. Not the young lady. But she was very much like her, very like. Am I going there now, sir? I must take my broom, sir. I must keep the steps clean. He was very good to me, very good.

'It's getting very dark, sir. Let me hold your hand.'

Allan Woodcourt took Jo's hands between his own. He prayed. It was the first prayer that Jo had ever heard. The boy's eyes closed and silence filled the poor room. Jo had moved on for the last time.

Jo had moved on for the last time.

14

Ada's Secret

Esther visits Richard again and takes Ada with her. Ada and Richard tell Esther their secret. Esther returns alone to Bleak House.

For some time, Esther had felt that her dear Ada had a secret which she was hiding from her. Ada was as sweet and loving as ever. But there was a sad look in her eyes that Esther did not understand.

One evening, Esther and Ada went up to bed after a quiet day at Bleak House. As they were saying goodnight, Esther saw that Ada's eyes were full of tears.

'Oh, my dear Esther,' said Ada, 'I wish I could speak to our guardian when we are all together. But I am afraid.'

'Why, my love?' Esther asked. 'Why are you afraid to speak to us? Is there anything wrong?'

'Oh, no, nothing wrong,' replied Ada. 'But after all his kindness! What shall I do? What shall I do?'

Ada hurried off to bed and said no more. When Ada had fallen asleep, Esther went in quietly to look at her. Ada seemed as beautiful as ever, but somehow changed. Esther noticed that Ada lay with one hand hidden under her pillow.

Esther was still very worried about Richard. Allan Woodcourt, who often visited Bleak House, told Esther more about Richard and his lawyer.

'This man is not helping Richard,' Allan told Esther. 'He has taken Richard's money and now he is trying to take Ada's too. Perhaps you should go and see Richard again. He will not listen to John Jarndyce. Richard thinks that his guardian is his worst enemy.'

Esther asked Ada to go with her to visit Richard. Ada did not want to go at first, but at last she agreed.

Esther thought that the London streets were darker and dirtier than ever. They found the door with Richard's name on it. Ada did not knock and the two girls went straight into the room.

Richard was sitting at a table looking at bundles of dusty papers. Jarndyce and Jarndyce was written on every paper.

Richard's face was very white, but he smiled when he saw Ada and Esther.

'If you had come earlier, you would have found Woodcourt here,' Richard told Esther. 'He is a good friend and always makes me feel happier. I get so tired sometimes. This is tiring work, but I know we shall win in the end. My dear Ada gives me hope.'

At these words, Ada got up and walked quickly over to Richard. She put her hand in Richard's and turned to face Esther.

'Esther, dear,' she said, very quietly. 'I am not going back to Bleak House with you. This is my home now. I have been married for two months and Richard is my dear husband.'

Richard held his wife close. Esther knew that nothing would change the love between the two cousins.

'Esther, my dear, will Cousin John ever forgive[5] me?'

'Of course he will,' Esther replied. 'He loves you both dearly.'

Ada took a ring from a chain round her neck. Richard, with a look of great love, put the ring on his wife's finger. Then, of course, Esther knew why Ada's hand had been hidden under her pillow. She had always worn her wedding-ring at night.

Esther went back to Bleak House alone.

John Jarndyce looked at Esther's face with his usual care.

'Esther dear,' he said, 'you have been crying.' He looked at the chair where Ada always sat in the evenings.

'Is Ada married, my dear?'

Esther told John Jarndyce all she knew. She told him how Ada and Richard had asked for their guardian's forgiveness.

Richard put the ring on his wife's finger.

'They have no need to ask for forgiveness,' said John Jarndyce. 'May Heaven bless them both. Poor Richard. Poor Ada. Bleak House is fast becoming empty.'

'I will always be here,' said Esther. 'I will do all I can to make Bleak House a happy place.'

'I am sure you will, Esther my love,' her guardian answered. But he looked sad and said no more about his letter to Esther. He had asked Esther to marry him and she had agreed, but no more had been said. There was no date for the wedding. Was it because Allan Woodcourt came so often to Bleak House?

15

Work For Mr Bucket

Mr Tulkinghorn warns Lady Dedlock that her disgrace is near. The lawyer is found murdered. Mr Bucket makes an arrest.

The Dedlocks were in London again. Their great house was always full of fashionable people. Lady Dedlock was as beautiful and as proud as ever. Mr Tulkinghorn was in London too. He was often seen at the Dedlocks' great house. He was always listening, but he said nothing. Lady Dedlock had sent her pretty young servant, Rosa, back home to her family. She did not want her own disgrace to harm this young girl. When Mr Tulkinghorn heard about this he was angry – very angry. The lawyer spoke to Lady Dedlock alone.

'I am surprised by what you have done, Lady Dedlock. You have sent that girl, Rosa, away. We agreed that nothing must be changed. You are not to be trusted, Lady Dedlock. You have broken your promise.'

'Are you going to tell Sir Leicester my story tonight?' Lady Dedlock asked slowly.

Mr Tulkinghorn shook his head.

'No, not tonight.'

'Tomorrow?'

'It may be tomorrow. I do not know. You are prepared. I wish you goodnight.'

'Are you going home now?' said Lady Dedlock.

'I am going home.'

Lady Dedlock bowed her head. Mr Tulkinghorn went out into the streets of London. He heard many voices and saw many people. He passed by shops, a few still open and full of light.

It was a fine night, a bright night, and Lady Dedlock could not stay inside her house. She called for a cloak[3]. She told a servant that she was going to walk alone in a nearby garden.

The moon had risen now. It shone on streets that had become silent, on churches, houses, dirty trees. In Lincoln's Inn, all was silent. No. What was that? Was it a shot? Where was it? A dog barked and doors opened.

Mr Tulkinghorn was at home. Did he hear the noise? His windows and doors remained shut.

In a few hours, daylight came to Lincoln's Inn. London began another busy day. Someone went as usual to clean Mr Tulkinghorn's rooms. Someone screamed, shouted, ran out into the street. What did it mean?

Mr Tulkinghorn's rooms remained dark that day. Mr Tulkinghorn had many visitors but he learnt nothing from them. For Mr Tulkinghorn had been found lying on the floor, shot through the heart.

———

Soon everyone knew. about Mr Tulkinghorn's dreadful death. Sir Leicester Dedlock asked Mr Bucket to find and catch the murderer. Mr Bucket, who knew as many secrets as the dead man, went from London to Chesney Wold and back again to London.

Sir Leicester and Mr Bucket went to Mr Tulkinghorn's funeral. Lady Dedlock did not. Hundreds of people stood in the streets to watch the carriages go by.

Mr Bucket was now staying at the Dedlocks' London house. He had his own key and went in and out whenever he wanted.

Strange letters had been sent to Mr Bucket, but he had shown them to no one. All these letters had been written by one person. In all of them were written only two words: LADY DEDLOCK.

Sir Leicester, who had been greatly troubled by his lawyer's death, became ill again. But he saw Mr Bucket every day.

One evening, Sir Leicester was sitting in the library as usual.

Mr Bucket came in and quietly closed the door behind him.

'Sir Leicester Dedlock,' he said, 'I have now completed this case. I have the facts. I know the name of the murderer.'

'Is the man already in prison?' asked Sir Leicester.

'It was a woman.'

Sir Leicester sat back in his chair, a dreadful look on his proud face.

'This will be a shock to you, Sir Leicester Dedlock,' Mr Bucket went on. 'Now, first of all, Lady Dedlock . . .'

Sir Leicester stared angrily at Mr Bucket.

'Please do not use my Lady's name, Mr Bucket,' said Sir Leicester.

Mr Bucket shook his head.

'But I must,' he said. 'What I have to say is about her Ladyship.'

Mr Bucket looked carefully at Sir Leicester's angry eyes.

'Sir Leicester, I must tell you that Mr Tulkinghorn knew that Lady Dedlock had a secret.'

'If he had told me anything about it, which he never did, I would have killed him myself,' Sir Leicester cried.

Mr Bucket shook his head.

'Before Lady Dedlock married you, she had a lover – that was her secret. The man should have married her, no doubt about that.

'Lady Dedlock saw her lover's writing on some law papers which Mr Tulkinghorn brought to your house. Soon afterwards, the man died, very poor. Lady Dedlock dressed herself as a servant and went to the place where her lover was buried. I can prove that this is true.

'I believe that Lady Dedlock and Mr Tulkinghorn spoke about this on the night Mr Tulkinghorn was killed. I know that Lady Dedlock went out that night. How do we know that she did not go down to Lincoln's Inn?'

Sir Leicester cried out and covered his face with his hands.

Mr Bucket looked at his watch.

'The person I shall arrest for this murder is in your house now. I am going to arrest her in front of you. There will be no noise or trouble.'

Mr Bucket rang for a servant, spoke to him outside the door for a moment and came into the room again.

There was silence for a minute or two. Sir Leicester sat without moving, his eyes fixed on the door.

The door slowly opened. A woman walked into the room. It was Mademoiselle Hortense, the Frenchwoman.

Mr Bucket moved quietly, shut the door and stood with his back against it.

The Frenchwoman looked round and saw Sir Leicester. 'I'm sorry,' she said. 'They told me there was no one here.'

She turned to leave the room. Mr Bucket was standing in front of the door.

'What trick are you playing on me?' she asked. 'Let me go downstairs.'

'Now Mademoiselle, you know who I am. Everyone knows Mr Bucket. I must arrest[2] you on a charge[2] of murder.'

'You are a devil,' said the Frenchwoman.

'If I were you,' said Mr Bucket, 'I would say nothing. You know, Sir Leicester, that this woman was dismissed from your house. She hated Lady Dedlock and told everyone so.'

'You are a devil,' said the Frenchwoman again.

'Now, my dear,' said Mr Bucket, 'I have told you. We know what you did. We know everything that you did that night. We have found the gun that you used and tried to throw away.'

'Lies,' said Mademoiselle, 'all lies.'

'You were the one who sent those letters,' went on Mr Bucket. 'You hate Lady Dedlock and you tried to disgrace her.'

Sir Leicester half-rose from his chair, but he was too ill to stand up.

'Now, Sir Leicester Dedlock,' Mr Bucket went on. 'We'll

just do this and this . . .' and before the Frenchwoman could do anything, he had closed the hand-cuffs on her wrists.

Mr Bucket walked to the door taking the Frenchwoman with him.

'You are very clever,' said Mademoiselle Hortense. 'But can you bring the dead man back? Can you give Sir Leicester his pride back? Can you help Lady Dedlock to forget her disgrace? No. Then you can do what you like with me.'

Sir Leicester Dedlock, left alone in the library, sat for some minutes without moving. At last he got up very slowly and looked round the empty room. He walked a few steps, stopped and then seemed to see someone in front of him.

Sir Leicester thought that Lady Dedlock stood before him. He saw her with her pride gone, disgraced and ruined. He cried out her name and dropped to the ground.

Mr Bucket makes an arrest.

16

Flight and Pursuit

Lady Dedlock writes a letter and flies from her disgrace. Mr Bucket and Esther follow her.

My Lady Dedlock was sitting in her own room. It was the room in which she had last spoken to Mr Tulkinghorn. She was sitting where she had sat that night. She was looking at the place where Mr Tulkinghorn had stood.

A few minutes earlier, a servant had brought Lady Dedlock a letter. She took it from the table and looked at it again. Three words were written on the paper: LADY DEDLOCK – MURDERESS.

The letter fell from Lady Dedlock's hand. Mr Tulkinghorn had been her enemy and she had often wished him dead. He was dead now, but he was still her enemy. Lady Dedlock remembered how she had stood outside his door that dreadful night. She remembered how she had wished to kill him.

Lady Dedlock put away the letter and rang the bell.

'Where is Sir Leicester?' she asked the servant.

'In the library, my Lady.'

'Is anyone with him?'

'No, my Lady, but Mr Bucket was with him earlier.' The servant left the room.

Everything was known. Her husband knew her disgrace. Mr Bucket thought she had murdered Mr Tulkinghorn.

Lady Dedlock, that proud woman, threw herself on the floor. She had wished Mr Tulkinghorn dead. Now his death had ruined her life. There was only one thing left for her to do.

Lady Dedlock sat down and wrote a letter to her husband:

People call me murderess. Believe me, I am innocent. I followed him home that night but his rooms were silent and dark. I came back.

Everything else you hear about me is true.

I have no home now. I have disgraced your great name too much. Try to forget the unhappy and wicked woman who now leaves you.

Goodbye.

Lady Dedlock dressed quickly and covered her face with a heavy veil. She left all her money and jewels in her room and she hurried downstairs. She waited until the great hall was empty. Then she opened the door and shut it quietly after her. Lady Dedlock walked away quickly into the dark, cold night. She did not look back.

———

Sir Leicester lay on the ground where he had fallen. His servants found him and laid him on his bed. He was a very sick old man who could not speak a word.

Sir Leicester moved his hands to show that he wanted a pencil. With the greatest difficulty he wrote, "My Lady . . .?"

A servant answered him.

'My lady went out, Sir Leicester, before we found you. She has not come back, but she left you this letter.'

Lady Dedlock's letter was placed in her husband's hand. He read it with the greatest difficulty – once, twice.

For an hour, Sir Leicester lay without moving. Then he moved his hands again. He wanted the pencil. "Mr B . . . " was all he wrote, but the servant understood. Very soon, Mr Bucket was standing beside Sir Leicester's bed.

'Sir Leicester, I am sorry to see you like this.'

Sir Leicester tried to put Lady Dedlock's letter into Mr Bucket's hand. He wrote: "Forgive . . . Find . . ."

Mr Bucket understood.

'Sir Leicester, I'll find her. The search will begin at once.'

Sir Leicester pointed to a box. There was money in it – a lot of money. Mr Bucket took what he needed and hurried from the room.

Mr Bucket went first to Lady Dedlock's bedroom. He looked round carefully. Lady Dedlock had left many beautiful and valuable things behind.

Mr Bucket opened a drawer and found a box. Inside the box there were some gloves and a handkerchief. On the handkerchief was the name: Esther Summerson. It was the same handkerchief which Esther had left on the face of Jenny's dead baby.

Oh, said Mr Bucket to himself, I'll take this with me. He took nothing else and left the great house at once.

Mr Bucket knew – was there anything that he didn't know? – that John Jarndyce and Esther Summerson were in London at that time. He took a coach to their house and knocked loudly at the front door. John Jarndyce, who was just going to bed, opened the door with some surprise.

'Don't be afraid, sir. I'm Inspector Bucket. Police. Look at this handkerchief, sir. It belongs to Miss Esther Summerson. I found it in a drawer of Lady Dedlock's. You know Lady Dedlock?'

'Yes.'

'There's been a discovery there today. Sir Leicester is dreadfully ill and Lady Dedlock has written this letter and run away. Here, read it.'

Mr Jarndyce read the letter. He could not believe that it had been written by the proud Lady Dedlock.

'She may try to kill herself,' said Mr Bucket. 'I have been sent to find her and give her Sir Leicester's forgiveness. I must have Miss Summerson. If I go alone, Lady Dedlock will be afraid of me. If I take Miss Summerson, she will know I am a friend.'

'Don't be afraid, sir. I'm Inspector Bucket. Police.'

John Jarndyce wasted no time. Very soon, Esther was dressed and ready to go with Mr Bucket.

Mr Bucket waited in the darkness, asking himself many questions. Where was Lady Dedlock now? Was she alive or dead? He looked at the handkerchief in his hand. They would go to the miserable cottage where Esther had left the handkerchief. Would they find my Lady there?

Another second, and Esther Summerson was ready. After Mr Bucket had asked her a few questions he said, 'Now, Miss, are you warmly dressed? This may be a long journey. It's a cold night for a young lady to be out.'

'My mother is somewhere out in the cold and snow,' Esther answered quietly. 'We must find her.'

'That's right, Miss,' said Inspector Bucket. 'All will end well. Now, Miss, we are off, if you are ready.'

17

Found

Lady Dedlock is found.

The journey, through darkness and snow, seemed to Esther like a dreadful dream. The coach drove quickly through the dark streets. They often stopped at police stations where Mr Bucket asked questions.

Soon they had left the streets of London far behind and were driving through open country. The snow was coming down more heavily now. Mr Bucket asked questions at every inn they passed. After a time, he heard news of a woman walking alone through the snow.

'It's all right, Miss,' he told Esther. 'She's in front of us. She passed this way earlier. We're near to Bleak House now, as you can probably see. We'll ask there.'

But Mr Bucket learnt nothing from the servants at Bleak House. In a short time, the coach stopped outside the brickmakers' cottages. It was now very late, but there was still a light in one of the rooms.

Esther knocked on the door and it was opened by a woman.

'I have come many miles through snow and darkness to find a lady,' said Esther. 'Has anyone been here?'

'There ain't no ladies here, as you can see,' answered one of the men rudely.

'Then is Jenny here?' said Esther.

'She's gone up to London,' said Jenny's husband. 'Yes, a lady was here and she talked to Jenny. What she said, I don't know. Now they've both gone – one to London and one to the north. That's all I'm saying.'

Esther and Mr Bucket at the brickmaker's cottage.

That was enough for Mr Bucket.

'Come, Miss,' he said to Esther, 'there's more to find out, I'm sure. Our way is to the north, following Lady Dedlock. She took no money, so she must be walking. We'll soon catch up with her.'

The coach drove on again and the snow fell harder'. Esther thought of her poor mother walking sad and alone in this dreadful weather.

They heard more news of a woman, just a little way in front of them. Once Mr Bucket stopped the coach, made Esther get out and ordered food and drink for her at an inn. Esther ate very little, but she sat by a fire while Mr Bucket asked his usual questions. He came back after some time looking very excited.

'What is it?' cried Esther. 'Have you found her?'

'No, no. Nobody's here, but I understand it all now. Remember, Miss Summerson, I'm Mr Bucket and you can trust me.'

He shouted to the driver.

'Back to London,' cried Mr Bucket. 'Quick, quick.'

'To London?' said Esther. 'Are we going back?'

'Yes, Miss, back as fast as we came. I'll follow her, I'll follow the poor woman.'

'Do not forget my poor mother,' Esther cried. 'Do not leave her on a night like this.'

'You are right, my dear, I won't. But I'll follow the other one. Now don't be afraid. Trust Inspector Bucket. Off we go then,' he called to the coachman.

About five o'clock in the morning, the coach was once more driving through the streets of London.

Esther was cold and afraid. She had almost fainted, when suddenly the coach stopped. They were in a London street that Esther seemed to know.

'Now my dear,' said Mr Bucket, 'if you will just get out, Miss, I think we're going to find this person with no trouble at all. But you must walk a little way now. The streets here are too narrow for the coach.'

Esther got out of the coach and looked around her.

'This street looks like Chancery Lane,' she said in surprise.

'And so it is, my dear,' said Mr Bucket, taking Esther by the arm.

The church clocks struck half past five. There were few people about so early in the morning. But a man was coming towards them, dressed in a warm cloak. He stopped and spoke Esther's name. The man was Allan Woodcourt.

'My dear Miss Summerson. Surely you should not be out in such weather. May I walk with you? Please take my cloak.'

The young doctor knew Inspector Bucket well. In a few quiet words, Esther told Allan Woodcourt the reason for her journey. Allan Woodcourt, without a word, took a dirty piece of paper from his pocket. It had been folded like a letter.

'Perhaps this has something to do with your journey,' Allan said. 'I could not understand it before. It was left at Mr Snagsby's shop by a poor woman. I had to call there and Mr Snagsby gave it to me. It is addressed to you, Miss Summerson. I was on my way to take it to you.'

'Whose writing is that?' said Mr Bucket quietly to Esther.

'It is my mother's.'

'Read the letter to me, please, Miss Summerson.'

The letter had been written at different times.

Esther began to read: *I came to the brickmaker's cottage, hoping to hear something about Esther. I wanted to lose anybody who might follow me. Do not blame the brickmaker's wife. She tried to help me.*

Then there was more writing, from another time:

I have now walked for many hours. I know I shall die in these dreadful streets. The cold and wet and my great unhappiness must surely kill me.

And then again – written much later:

I have done all I can to lose myself. No one can find me now. My husband will be saved from more disgrace. I hope this letter will reach my child at last. If I can walk so far, I am going to a place from which I shall never return. I shall die – near him. Goodbye. Forgive me.

Esther nearly fainted again.

'Come, Miss,' said Mr Bucket, 'it's nearly over now. And you, sir,' he said to Mr Woodcourt, 'hold her other arm. I know where to go now.'

Esther was so tired that she did not see the dark and dirty streets. At last they stood by an iron gate. The gate was closed. Behind it was the miserable burial ground where Jo had taken Lady Dedlock. It was the place where Nemo had been buried.

Esther looked up as they stopped. She gave a cry. There, on the steps, was a poor woman. She lay on the wet steps without moving. One hand was holding on to a bar of the iron gate. Esther ran towards her.

'It's Jenny, the brickmaker's wife. She is ill. I must help her.'

Mr Bucket put out his hand to hold Esther back.

'You still do not understand. They changed clothes at the cottage.'

Esther repeated Mr Bucket's words, but she did not understand them. She looked again at the poor woman on the steps. She moved slowly towards her. This time, Mr Bucket did not stop Esther. She moved up to the gate and bent down. Esther lifted the woman's head, held back the long, dark hair and gently turned the face.

It was the face of Esther's own mother, Lady Dedlock, cold and dead.

The face of Esther's own mother, Lady Dedlock,
cold and dead.

18

Allan Woodcourt Speaks

Sir Leicester returns to Chesney Wold. Esther and John Jarndyce go to London to be near Ada and Richard.

Bleak House was still empty. Esther and John Jarndyce had decided to stay in London for a time to be near Ada.

Esther visited Ada every day. The money Ada had given to Richard had nearly all gone. Richard spent most of the day in Court now. He could think of nothing but Jarndyce and Jarndyce. Esther sat with Ada during the day and tried to comfort her.

In this way, Esther gradually forgot the pain of her mother's death. Sir Leicester had shut up his London house and had gone to live at Chesney Wold. He would never be well enough to live in London again. Indeed, he did not wish to. He was content to live at Chesney Wold and remember Lady Dedlock in her happier days.

Allan Woodcourt often visited Richard, both as a friend and as a doctor. Richard had no real illness, but every day he became thinner and paler. All Richard's friends were becoming very worried about him. Although Ada was very worried too, she was always bright and happy in front of Richard.

One day Ada talked to Esther about Richard.

'No one understands Richard better than I do. I know that he is getting worse every day. But when he comes home, I want him to see no unhappiness in my face.'

Ada stopped for a moment and then went on.

'My love for Richard helps me, Esther, and now I have something else to help me. I am expecting a child. I hope that one day this child will help its father. Perhaps a beautiful daughter or a fine son will help Richard to forget this wicked Chancery. I cannot do it. But, my dearest Esther, a great fear fills my heart.'

'What is it, Ada?'

'It is the fear that my dear husband will not live to see his child.'

Richard came back from Court at that moment and Ada quickly dried her tears. Richard had met Allan Woodcourt and had brought him home for dinner.

When they sat down to the simple meal, Esther watched Richard closely. Sometimes he laughed with Allan, but at other times Richard sat silent and sad. His young face had a dreadful, tired look.

After dinner, Ada played some old songs on the piano and Allan sat beside Richard. The young doctor's friendly conversation brought back a happier look to Richard's face.

Esther stayed late that night because she had some sewing to finish for Ada. When she was ready to go, Allan Woodcourt said he would walk home with her.

On the way home, they spoke of Richard and Ada. Esther tried to thank Allan for what he had done to help them.

When they reached the house, they went upstairs to look for John Jarndyce. But he was not at home. Allan began to speak and, in a moment, Esther knew that he loved her.

As she listened, Esther had only one thought: Too late, too late. She had promised to marry John Jarndyce.

'I did not speak to you when I first came back,' Allan went on, 'because I was still a poor man. I know now that I shall always be poor. I also know that you are the only woman I could ever marry.'

'Oh, Mr Woodcourt,' cried Esther, 'Mr Woodcourt, it is a great thing to win love. I am proud to have won yours. But I cannot accept your love, I am not free. Believe me, dear Mr Woodcourt, I shall never forget this night. I shall remember your words with pride and joy for ever.'

Allan could not speak. He took Esther's hand and kissed it.

'Mr Woodcourt,' Esther went on, 'you will be glad to know that the future is clear and bright before me. I have promised to marry the man who has looked after me for so long. I cannot leave him. I have promised to stay with him.'

'You are speaking of Mr Jarndyce,' said Allan Woodcourt. 'I hope your lives together will be happy. Goodnight, dearest Esther, goodbye.'

When Allan Woodcourt had left her, Esther stood in the darkened room. She cried. Esther knew she must marry John Jarndyce. She also knew that Allan's words of love would always stay in her heart.

The next day Esther spoke to John Jarndyce about his letter. She promised to marry him the following month.

19

The Will

An important Jarndyce will is found. The will gives Richard new hope. John Jarndyce takes Esther to the new Bleak House where Allan Woodcourt is waiting for her.

One day about two weeks later, Mr Bucket came to see Mr Jarndyce in his London home.

'Mr Jarndyce and Miss Summerson,' said the Inspector. 'I'm sorry to trouble you, but I have important news. Do you remember Mr Krook, the strange old man in the Rag and Bottle Shop? Well, Mr Jarndyce, that old man has died, died of drink as far as we can tell. His shop was full of old papers. The old man could not read them, but he threw nothing away.

'I had a look through these papers. I found an old paper with the name of Jarndyce on it. It is a will.'

Mr Bucket held out the paper in his hand. John Jarndyce did not take it.

'I thank you, Mr Bucket. But I will not look at that paper. The whole case of Jarndyce and Jarndyce makes my heart sick.'

'If it is a will,' said Esther, 'it may give money to Ada and Richard.'

'If the paper can help them,' said John Jarndyce, 'then the lawyers must know about it. I will take it to Lincoln's Inn at once.'

Mr Jarndyce went at once to his lawyer, who was most surprised. Mr Jarndyce had not been near him for many years.

The lawyer read the paper carefully. He began to look very interested.

'Mr Jarndyce,' he said, 'have you read this?'

'Certainly not, sir.'

'My dear sir,' said the lawyer, 'this is a will of a very recent date. In fact it is more recent than any other. And it is all perfectly correct.'

'Well,' said John Jarndyce, 'what has that to do with me?'

'I will tell you,' said the lawyer. 'This will gives Mr Richard Carstone and Miss Ada Clare, now Mrs Richard Carstone, a great deal of money, a very great deal.'

'Can any good come from Jarndyce and Jarndyce? I cannot believe it,' said John Jarndyce. 'What must be done now?'

'The new Term[2], Mr Jarndyce, begins next month. We must get ready at once. The case must come before the Court as soon as possible.'

When Richard heard about the will, he was filled with new hope. With the lawyers, he worked harder than ever before to prepare his case. He looked forward eagerly to a better life for Ada and the coming child.

Meanwhile, Esther was preparing for her marriage to John Jarndyce. Just at this time, Mr Jarndyce left London. He went up to Yorkshire to help Allan Woodcourt. The young doctor was going to work among the poor people in a small village there.

Esther was very surprised to receive a letter from her guardian. He asked Esther to join him in Yorkshire at once.

It was night when Esther reached the end of her journey and her guardian was waiting for her.

'You must be wondering why I have brought you here, my dear Esther,' John Jarndyce said kindly. 'I will tell you at once.

'I have wanted to help Allan Woodcourt for a long time. He was very good to Jo and is very kind to our dear Ada and Richard. I have found a little house for Allan near here. But I want advice. So I have brought the best housekeeper I know to give me that advice. And here she is, laughing and crying together.'

'I will do my best to help you,' said Esther. 'It is always a pleasure to help you, my dear Guardian.'

101

The next day was beautifully sunny. After breakfast, Esther and her guardian went out together. They were soon walking through the garden of a pretty little house. Esther saw with surprise that the garden was arranged exactly like her own at Bleak House.

They walked up the path to the back door of the pretty little house. Inside the cottage, everything was neatly arranged. Everything was exactly as Esther liked it. She cried out in surprise.

'And now, dear Esther,' said John Jarndyce when they had seen everything in the cottage, 'last of all, the name of this house. Come and see.'

They went outside and over the front door was written: "Bleak House."

John Jarndyce took Esther to a seat in the garden and they sat down.

'Listen to me, my child, but say nothing yet. When I asked you to marry me, I thought I could make you happy. But then Allan Woodcourt came home. I soon knew that he should be my dear Esther's husband. I had no doubt at all.'

Esther held down her head.

'I am your father now, my child. Don't cry. This is a day of joy. Allan Woodcourt stood beside your father when he lay dead. He stood beside your dead mother. Today, I give you to him with a father's love. May you live together for many happy years.'

They were no longer alone. Allan Woodcourt was standing by Esther's side. She stood up and looked into the eyes of her future husband.

What a happy day that was for the three friends. They spoke about the past and looked forward to the future with the greatest joy. Esther and Allan agreed to marry as soon as possible. They were going to live in the new Bleak House and make it as happy as the old one. But they did not forget Ada and Richard. Their future had to be decided first. And only the Court of Chancery could make that decision.

'Last of all, the name of this house. Come and see.'

Richard Begins His Life Again

The end of the case of Jarndyce and Jarndyce. Richard begins his new life.

Esther, Allan and John Jarndyce went back to London the next day. The new Term had just begun and the case of Jarndyce and Jarndyce was coming before the Court.

On the day of the case, Esther and Allan went together to the Court of Chancery. The streets were very busy that day and they arrived a little late. To their surprise, there was a large crowd waiting outside the door and the Court itself was full. Esther and Allan were not able to see or to hear what was going on inside. Suddenly there was a burst of laughter and loud cry of "Silence". Then the doors opened and a number of lawyers came out, laughing together.

'What case is on?' Allan Woodcourt asked the lawyers.

'Jarndyce and Jarndyce of course,' said one of the lawyers, 'but it's over now.'

'Over for the day?' Esther asked.

'No, over for ever.' And the lawyers laughed again.

Was it possible? Had the case been decided after so long? Had the will made Ada and Richard rich at last?

In a few minutes, the crowd came pouring out of the Court. Some people were bringing out great bundles of papers. Everyone was laughing.

At last, Esther saw John Jarndyce's lawyer coming towards them.

'What has happened today?' said Esther.

'Jarndyce and Jarndyce is over now.'

'Happened? Well, not much has actually happened today. But the case is over.'

'But what about the will?'

'Ah yes, the will. The will was not discussed. You must understand,' said the lawyer, 'that this case has been going on for a long time, a very long time. Only the best lawyers have been working on it. These things must be paid for, you know, they must be paid for.'

'Excuse me, sir,' said Allan, 'I think I understand you. The money has all gone. It has been taken by the costs[1] of the case?'

'That is so.'

'And that means that there can be no case and that all is lost?'

'That is so,' said the lawyer with a bow.

'My dear,' said Allan to Esther quietly, 'this will break Richard's heart.'

'If you want Mr Carstone, sir, I left him in the Court. He seemed a little shocked by the news. Good-day, sir.'

And the lawyer hurried away.

'My dear love,' said Allan, 'leave me to look after Richard. Go home and tell your guardian what has happened. Come to Ada later.'

Esther hurried home and told John Jarndyce everything.

In the afternoon, Esther and her guardian went together to Richard's rooms. Allan had found Richard sitting in a corner of the courtroom. He could not move and his mouth was filled with blood. Allan Woodcourt had brought him home.

Esther went inside the room. Richard had been asking for her. Richard was lying on a sofa with his eyes closed. Allan was sitting beside him. Richard opened his eyes and saw Esther.

'Kiss me, my dear,' he said. 'I am happy, so happy to hear about your marriage. Allan will look after you so well.'

Esther and Allan talked about the future as much as they could. They wanted to give Richard hope for his own life too.

John Jarndyce came quietly into the room and laid his hand on Richard's.

'Oh, sir,' said Richard, 'you are a good man. I know it now.'

'My dear Richard. How are you, my dear boy?'

'I am very weak at present, sir, but I hope to be stronger. I must begin my life again.'

'That's right,' John Jarndyce replied. He knew that Richard was dying.

'I have learnt my lesson now,' Richard went on. 'It was a hard lesson, but I have learnt it at last. I have been thinking. When Esther and Allan marry, I should like to live in the new Bleak House. With my dear Ada there too, I'm sure I would get better quickly.'

Richard turned to Ada.

'I have brought you much sadness, my own love. My life has fallen across your life like a shadow. Our marriage has made you poor and unhappy. You will forgive me, Ada, when I begin my life again?'

A smile spread across Richard's face as Ada bent to kiss him. His eyes closed for the last time. Richard began his new life – in another world.

That night, when Miss Flite heard the news of Richard's death, she let all her birds fly away.

21

Later On

The end of the story. Esther and her friends find happiness.

Seven years had passed since the death of Richard Carstone. Ada had a beautiful boy. His name was Richard too. The child loved Esther dearly and called her his second mother.

Allan and Esther were happily married and the proud parents of two little daughters. After a time, a room had been added to the new Bleak House. It was for John Jarndyce whenever he came to stay with them.

Allan and Esther never became rich, but they always had enough money. The poor people of the district loved their doctor and his wife.

One night, Allan came home late to Bleak House. He was surprised to see Esther still sitting in the garden.

'My dear Esther, what are you doing out here so late?' Allan asked his wife.

'The moon is shining so brightly and the night is so beautiful. I was sitting here thinking,' said Esther with a smile.

'What were you thinking about, my dear?'

'I was thinking about how I looked before my illness. I sometimes wish that I had my good looks once again.'

'My dear wife, don't you ever look in the glass?'

'Of course I do,' cried Esther.

'You must know then,' said Allan, taking his dear wife in his arms, 'that you are more beautiful than you ever were!'

'I know my children are very pretty,' said Esther slowly, 'and my dear Ada and her child are beautiful. I know that my husband is very handsome and that my guardian is the kindest in the world. And if you, my dear Allan, say I am beautiful . . .'

And Esther led her husband into their happy home – Bleak House.

POINTS
FOR
UNDERSTANDING

Points for Understanding

1

1 What case was before the Court of Chancery?
2 Why had the lawyers lost interest in this case?
3 Where were Ada Clare and Richard Carstone going to live?
4 Who was going with them?
5 Why did Miss Flite go to the Court of Chancery every day?
6 Miss Flite said: 'I'm mad, quite mad.' What made her mad?
7 Who was Jo?

2

1 When were footsteps heard on the Ghost's Walk?
2 'Nothing important has been decided,' said Mr Tulkinghorn.
   Who was Mr Tulkinghorn? What was he talking about?
3 Lady Dedlock asked two questions about the handwriting on the
   law papers. What were the questions? What was the difference in
   the way in which she asked them?
4 Why did Mr Tulkinghorn want to find the man who had written
   the papers?

3

1 What was special about Krook's Rag and Bottle shop?
2 Why was Krook called the Lord Chancellor?
3 When would Miss Flite's birds go free?
4 What is strange about the name 'Nemo'?
5 Mrs Jellyby was too busy to look after her own children. Why?
6 Why did Mr Tulkinghorn go to Krook's shop?
7 Why was Mr Tulkinghorn going to tell Lady Dedlock about the
   death of Nemo?

4

1 A maid brought Esther the housekeeping keys. Why was Esther pleased?
2 Why had John Jarndyce decided to look after Esther?
3 What was the case of Jarndyce and Jarndyce about?
4 Why did Tom Jarndyce call his home 'Bleak House'?
5 Richard lay awake for a long time thinking of the future. What did he think of particularly?
6 Ada and Esther went with Mrs Pardiggle to the brickmakers' cottages. But they did not want to. Why?
7 What did Esther use to cover the face of the dead child?

5

1 What was Tom-All-Alone's?
2 Why did people ask Jo questions about Nemo?
3 People like Mrs Jellyby helped the poor people of Africa. Why did Dickens think this was not a good thing?
4 The lady who spoke to Jo said that she was a servant. Did Jo believe her?
5 What two places did the lady want to see?

6

1 Why was John Jarndyce worried about Richard Carstone?
2 What was the reason for the small dinner-party at Bleak House?
3 Who was the guest at the dinner party?
4 Why was Richard Carstone going to London?
5 What did Richard say which made Ada look unhappy?
6 Why did Ada and Esther decide to visit Richard in London?
7 Richard had decided not to become a doctor. What did he want to do instead?
8 What was Esther's earliest memory?
9 Who had asked John Jarndyce to be Esther's guardian?
10 What was Allan Woodcourt going to do?
11 Esther did not forget to take the flowers with her. What do you think this shows about Esther's feelings?

7

1 Why did Esther and Ada go to stay near Chesney Wold?
2 Why did Richard not go with them?
3 When Esther saw Lady Dedlock in church, she had a strange feeling. What did she remember?
4 How did Mr Jarndyce, Esther and Ada meet Lady Dedlock?
5 A carriage came for Lady Dedlock with two women in it. Who were they?
6 What did Lady Dedlock do to make Hortense so angry?

8

1 The policeman asked: 'How did a poor boy get two silver pieces?' How did Jo get this money?
2 What did Mr Snagsby tell Mr Tulkinghorn?
3 Why did Mr Bucket and Mr Snagsby go to visit Tom-All-Alone's?
4 Why did some people seem afraid of Mr Bucket?
5 Why had the brickmakers come to London?
6 Jo saw a lady in Mr Tulkinghorn's dark room. Who did he think she was?
7 Mr Bucket said: 'It was the other lady but she was wearing this woman's dress.' Who was 'the other lady'? Who was 'this woman'?

9

1 What was Richard Carstone's new plan?
2 Was John Jarndyce happy about Richard's new plan?
3 John Jarndyce said to Richard and Ada: 'From now on you must be cousins only.' What did he mean?

10

1 Jo said: 'She looks like the other lady.' What 'other lady' was he thinking of?
2 What could this terrible illness do to a woman?
3 Why had Esther's looking-glass been taken away?
4 Why did Richard Carstone no longer trust John Jarndyce?
5 What had happened to Miss Flite's family?

6 Why was Miss Flite worried about Richard Carstone?
7 What had happened to Allan Woodcourt?
8 Why did Esther think that Bleak House would be her home for the rest of her life?

11

1 What was Lady Dedlock holding in her hand?
2 Why must the fact that Lady Dedlock is Esther's mother be kept secret?
3 Who had looked after Esther when she was very young?
4 Why did Esther run in fear from the Ghost's Walk?

12

1 Who was the 'great lady' in Mr Tulkinghorn's story meant to be? Who was the servant meant to be?
2 Why did the girl's father in Tulkinghorn's story take his daughter away from the lady's house?
3 Why had Mr Tulkinghorn told this story?
4 Tulkinghorn said to Lady Dedlock, 'Do you promise?' What was he asking her to do?
5 Hortense said she was rich in hate. Who did she hate?
6 'I will come here again and again until you do what I want.' What was Tulkinghorn's reply?

13

1 What did John Jarndyce ask Esther in his letter?
2 What was Esther's reply?
3 Why did Esther become angry with Richard?
4 Esther thought that Allan Woodcourt looked at her sadly. What did she think he had noticed?
5 What did Allan Woodcourt promise Esther?
6 Why could Allan Woodcourt not ask Esther to marry him?
7 Why did Allan Woodcourt look at Jo with horror?
8 Jo said: 'She was very much like her, very like.' Why did Jo think that Esther was very like the lady who had given him money?

14

1 What was Ada's secret?
2 The date of Esther's marriage to John Jarndyce had not yet been decided on. What was possibly the reason for this?

15

1 Why had Lady Dedlock sent Rosa home to her family?
2 Why was Mr Tulkinghorn angry about this?
3 When was Mr Tulkinghorn going to tell Sir Leicester about Lady Dedlock's secret?
4 A dog barked. What noise had the animal heard?
5 What words were written in the letters sent to Mr Bucket?
6 What was the writer of the letter trying to say?
7 Mr Bucket said that Lady Dedlock had gone out on the night of the murder. Sir Leicester cried out and covered his face with his hands. What was he thinking?
8 Who had sent the letters to Mr Bucket?
9 Who had murdered Tulkinghorn?
10 What happened to Sir Leicester after Mr Bucket left?

16

1 What had Lady Dedlock wanted to do on the night Mr Tulkinghorn was murdered?
2 The servant told Lady Dedlock that Mr Bucket had been with Sir Leicester. What did Lady Dedlock immediately think?
3 Sir Leicester was able to write only two words: 'Forgive. . . Find . . .' What did Mr Bucket understand by these words?
4 Mr Bucket found a handkerchief in Lady Dedlock's room. Whose handkerchief was it? What did he do with it?
5 Why did Mr Bucket want Esther to go with him?

17

1 Mr Bucket decided to go to the north. Why?
2 Mr Bucket suddenly decided to go back to London. What had he understood?

3　In her letter to Esther Lady Dedlock wrote: 'I shall die – near him.' Who was 'him'?
4　Where did Mr Bucket go to find Lady Dedlock?

18

1　What great fear filled Ada's heart?
2　Esther had only one thought: 'Too late, too late.' What was too late? Why?
3　What answer did Esther give to Allan Woodcourt?

19

1　What paper had Mr Bucket found in Krook's shop?
2　How could this paper help Richard and Ada?
3　Why did John Jarndyce ask Esther to go and join him in Yorkshire?
4　What was the name of the house in Yorkshire?
5　What had John Jarndyce arranged without telling Esther?
6　Ada and Richard's future had to be decided first. What did their future depend upon?

20

1　What ended the case of Jarndyce and Jarndyce?
2　What did the news of the end of Jarndyce and Jarndyce do to Richard?
3　Why did Miss Flite let her birds fly away?

21

What reasons did Allan and Esther have for being happy?

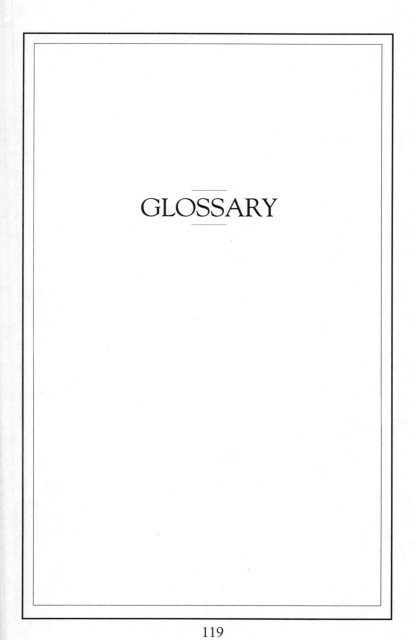

GLOSSARY

Glossary

SECTION 1
Note on the High Court of Chancery

The High Court of Chancery was the oldest and most important Court in England. Disagreements about the ownership of money or property were decided by the Court of Chancery. And the Court of Chancery often had to decide the exact meaning of a person's *will* – a paper which says what a person wants done with his property after his death. The case of Jarndyce and Jarndyce was about a will.

When a disagreement was taken to the Court it became one of the Court's *cases*. The Lord Chancellor gave a decision on each case. This decision was called his *judgement*. Before he gave a judgement, the Chancellor had to hear all the facts.

The *claimants* were the people who said that the money or property belonged to them. If the claimants were under the age of twenty-one and their parents were dead, they became *wards of court* and the Court decided who would look after them.

The claimants had to pay lawyers to speak for them in the Court. These lawyers were men trained to understand the law and argue about it in Court. Good lawyers had to be paid a lot of money.

The costs – the money paid for lawyers and for the business of the Court – were often very high especially if the case was a long one.

In *Bleak House*, Dickens used the case of Jarndyce and Jarndyce to show how the expenses and the long delays of the Court of Chancery made people poor and very unhappy. The High Court of Chancery was abolished in 1922.

121

SECTION 2
Other legal terms

arrest (page 83)

    if the police think that someone has broken the law, they arrest
that person and take him or her to a police station to question him.

charge (page 83)

    after a person has been arrested (see *arrest* above) and questioned,
that person must be charged if the police want to keep him or her
in the police station. The charge is a statement of what the police
say the arrested person has done wrong.

inquest (page 20)

    an inquest is held when a person dies and the reason for his death is
not known.

law-hand (page 11)

    a special kind of handwriting used to copy law papers.

law-stationer (page 47)

    a man who sold the special forms and papers used by lawyers.

Term (page 101)

    the length of time when the courts are held. There are three law
terms every year. Lawyers have a holiday or *vacation* between terms
and the *Long Vacation* is always in the summer.

Vacation – *Long Vacation* (page 47)

    See under *Term* above.

SECTION 3
Terms to do with life in nineteenth-century England

General note: In the middle of the nineteenth century when Dickens
wrote *Bleak House*, England was a very rich country. But many rich
people, like the Dedlocks, did not know – or perhaps did not care–
about the poor. In big cities like London, the rich people's houses were
sometimes near the poorest streets. But rich and poor did not meet.
The rich did not know that poor people died hungry and alone every
day.

burial-ground (page 29)
a place where very poor people were buried.
carriage (page 4)
very rich people travelled in their own carriages. Coaches were also used and people paid money for a seat in them.
changed (page 21)
on long coach journeys, horses became tired after a time and they had to be given a rest. New horses took their place and the journey continued.
cloak (page 81)
a long coat without sleeves, worn by men and women. It completely covered the person who was wearing it.
coach (page 72)
see *carriage* above.
crossing-sweeper (page 4)
a person who cleaned the dirty, muddy streets so that people could cross them easily.
keys – *housekeeping keys* (page 23)
every large house had many servants. The housekeeper told the servants what to do. She carried every key of the house with her. Esther was not a servant, but John Jarndyce wanted her to look after Bleak House for him.
move on (page 47)
poor people with nowhere to go and nowhere to sleep often became ill or caused trouble. The police told these people to move on to another town.
opium (page 20)
a drug which was often used as a medicine in the nineteenth century. Sometimes people died because they had taken too much.
servant – *lady's servant* (page 30)
every rich lady had her own special servant. The lady's servant knew how to dress and behave like a lady.
sewing (page 38)
making clothes by hand. Esther spent much of her time sewing.
veil (page 30)
a piece of very fine cloth used to cover a woman's face.

SECTION 4
Terms to do with family life

bridesmaid (page 35)
> when a girl gets married, her best friend is her bridesmaid and stands behind her in the church.

engagement (page 35)
> a promise between two people to marry one another.

great-uncle (page 24)
> the uncle of your father or of your mother.

guardian (page 24)
> someone who takes care of a young person whose parents have died.

orphan (page 24)
> someone whose parents are dead.

SECTION 5
General

bored (page 12)
> feeling tired and unhappy because you are not interested in anything.

bruised (page 26)
> marked on the face by hard blows.

creature – *poor creature* (page 8)
> a person we feel sorry for is often spoken of as a poor creature.

damp (page 28)
> a wetness in old buildings which are not heated properly.

disgrace (page 9)
> when a person did something wrong or shameful and it became known, that person was said to bring disgrace on themselves and their families.

forgive (page 77)
> to excuse someone we love when they have done something wrong or foolish.

landlord (page 15)
> a man who owns a house where people pay money to live in rooms. The people who live in the rooms are called *lodgers* and the room is called their *lodging*.

lodger (page 17)
    see *landlord* above.
lodging (page 14)
    see *landlord* above.
looking-glass (page 59)
    a mirror.
people – *fashionable people* (page 28)
    rich and well-known people.
ruined (page 4)
    a person who has lost everything in his life is ruined.
    (page 28)
    the houses were old and falling down. People should not have been
    living in them.
scars (page 59)
    the marks left on Esther's face after her illness (smallpox).
shipwreck (page 60)
    the sinking of a ship in a storm.
signs (page 60)
    changes in a person's face which Miss Flite can understand. She has
    seen these changes on the faces of many people made unhappy by
    Chancery.

Of Mice and Men *by John Steinbeck*
The Great Ponds *by Elechi Amadi*
Rebecca *by Daphne du Maurier*
Our Mutual Friend *by Charles Dickens*
The Grapes of Wrath *by John Steinbeck*
The Return of the Native *by Thomas Hardy*
Weep Not, Child *by Ngugi wa Thiong'o*
Precious Bane *by Mary Webb*
Mine Boy *by Peter Abrahams*

For further information on the full selection of Readers
at all five levels in the series, please refer to the Macmillan
Readers catalogue.

Published by Macmillan Heinemann ELT
Between Towns Road, Oxford OX4 3PP
Macmillan Heinemann ELT is an imprint of
Macmillan Publishers Limited
Companies and representatives throughout the world
Heinemann is a registered trademark of Harcourt Education, used under licence.

ISBN 1–405–07321–7
EAN 978–1–405073–21–9

This retold version by Margaret Tarner for Macmillan Readers
First published 1976
Text © Margaret Tarner 1976, 1992, 1998, 2002
Design and illustration © Macmillan Publishers Limited 2002

This edition first published 2005

Illustrated by Kay Dixie
Cover illustration by Angus Mewse

Printed in Thailand

2009 2008 2007 2006 2005
10 9 8 7 6 5 4 3 2 1